A YEAR ON EL ORO

An unlikely voyage aboard an extraordinary yacht

RICHARD DUMAS

LOVELYBANKS

Lovelybanks
PO Box 57,
Taralga,
NSW 2580

Taralga is the traditional land of the *Burra Burra* peoples of the Gundungurra Nation

A catalogue record for this book is available from the National Library of Australia

A YEAR ON EL ORO
ISBN 9781763581913 (PRINT BOOK)
ISBN 9781763581920 (EBOOK)

The paper in this book is FSC® certified. FSC® promotes environmentally responsible, socially beneficial and economically viable management of the world's forests.

For Tim and Sophie without whom none of this would have been possible. Also for my beautiful wife Til for agreeing to come!

PROLOGUE

'I am of the opinion that the boldest measures are the safest.'
— Horatio Nelson

It's the run up to Christmas and I'm working from home; scrolling through my inbox, the low buzz of blowflies insistent against the window. Buried among the spam, there's an email from Tim Wilson, asking me to lunch. It's a surprise as I don't know Tim well. He's a friend of Til's family and we've bumped into each other over the years. I've always liked him. It's hard not to, he's a likeable person. He's from the generation above, in his eighties, but he has a sparkle in his eyes and when he talks to you, he has a conspiratorial grin as if letting you in on a secret for your ears only. He also loves sailing, and we inevitably gravitate to that topic. The lunch clashes with some work thing so I politely decline and, in my note back, I mention it's a shame we're not catching up as I want to pick his brains about sailing in the Mediterranean. I know he keeps a boat there, and I've long harboured an ambition to sail those waters. An email comes pinging back. 'In that case,' he responds, 'I may have a proposition for you. Let's catch up for a coffee.'

Til and I are up in Sydney a week later and we catch up with Tim at the CYCA. He takes us down the floating concrete pontoon to show us his yacht. Nestled amidst the row of plastic, floating caravans, Lord Corky stands out as a narrow, low to the water, carbon fibre racing machine complete with daggerboards and canting keel. 'I'm going to have to get some electric winches' sighs Tim. 'All my friends are getting too geriatric to bring the sails in.'

A little later we're cradling takeaway coffees sitting on the wall above the marina, dangling our feet over the dark water; a smell of cut grass in the air, from the park behind us. 'I've got a bit of a problem,' Tim says, and he goes on to tell us about El Oro, a beautiful 68' timber ketch he bought in a rundown state in 2007. The boat was originally built for Baron Bich, of biro fame, and was made in France from cold-moulded, mahogany strip planking in the early 1970s. Two boats were built from the same design, and El Oro's sister ship Kriter came third in the first Whitbread round-the-world race. For some reason, Baron Bich decided he didn't want to pursue offshore sailing, focussing instead on the America's Cup where he put together the first ever challenge from outside the English-speaking world. Meanwhile, he gifted El Oro to his Financial Director. He must have been a good person to work for.

Tim is a surgeon, but he has his fingers in lots of different pies. One of these is Ringle Marine Services, a boatyard off the Yangon River in Burma specialising in restoring timber yachts. He established Ringle in the early 2000's and bought El Oro shortly after as a project for the yard and sailed her to Burma from Spain. 'We had a few challenges on that trip,' he chuckles as he tells us how he and his crew battled to keep the aging boat from falling apart as they crossed the Indian Ocean. The boat stayed in the yard for several years being used to train craftsmen and as a filler between other jobs. Eventually, after an extensive rebuild he brought her back to Europe and after another later stint in the boatyard, she was sailed across to America. Since then, he's campaigned her for a few seasons in the Caribbean and on the east coast of the US.

'My problem,' says Tim, 'is I left El Oro in Rhode Island in late 2019 expecting to re-launch her in 2020 for another season of racing.' He shakes his head, 'I haven't been able to get to her since.' Throughout the pandemic, El Oro has sat out of the water, unattended, shrink wrapped in white plastic sheeting, enduring freezing New England winters and baking summers for three long years.

'I probably ought to sell her,' says Tim wistfully. 'I've got too many boats. But who knows what condition she's in now.' He turns and looks directly at us. 'Would you and Til like to take her and have a play? You could borrow her for a year or so?' I must have stared at him open mouthed as he goes on. 'You'd be doing me a favour. She needs to be used.'

That was it. The offer that came out of the blue. It raises so many questions. Can we afford to take a year out? What about our careers? How difficult is this boat to sail and can we handle it? How many people are needed to operate it? Is it responsible to head-off into the blue at this stage of our lives? We have three children, the youngest about to finish school, and we both have aging parents.

We leave the discussion saying we'll think about it, but I know in my heart this is an offer that only comes round once, and I'll regret it for the rest of my life if we decline. I work for a wine business, and they have an office in Sydney on the forty second floor of a shiny tower block in Barangaroo, a revamped precinct in the heart of town. I'm not there very often as we live three hours away in the bush but it's usually a good opportunity to reconnect with my colleagues. This time, heading in after my meeting with Tim, it's impossible to concentrate on work. My mind is buzzing with the opportunity laid out before me, but I'm disconnected from everyone else, with a secret so outrageous that I can't share. Out of the window, far below, the magnificent harbour glistens blue in the midday sunshine. It's studded with boats of all descriptions; ferries, small working boats pulling laden barges and in amongst these, sailing yachts, gliding across the water. One is making towards the heads, out to the east and I watch as it disappears slowly behind the cliffs.

Til and I talk things over going round and round in circles. I have some sailing experience, having grown up with boats, but I've never sailed a yacht this large, let alone skippered it. I've also never taken a yacht across an ocean before. Til has less experience. At heart, she's a land person having spent her childhood on a farm in country New South Wales. We've been on a few charter holidays in the past and for a while when we lived in Sydney, we owned a small yacht built in the 1960s which we kept in Pittwater, and this was mainly used for twilight racing or for hosting floating picnics. It was always me doing the sailing, Til's job was producing the food and drinks, something she did magnificently. On the rare occasion we headed offshore, she was prone to seasickness. How will she manage living aboard for a year?

To my surprise, she's enthusiastic about the offer, although concerned about how we'll afford a year without working. 'But what about getting seasick?' I ask. 'It could be miserable.' She shrugs.

'It's mainly in the mind. I'm not going to get sick…'

Tim and I catch up for lunch a week or so later in a small restaurant in Potts Point to discuss things in more detail. We sit on the pavement, traffic grinding past us up the hill from

Woolloomooloo. 'How many people does it take to sail El Oro?' I ask, having seen video footage of 1970's ocean racers packed with dozens of crew.

'Oh, I think you should be able to manage with two,' says Tim smiling disingenuously. 'That's the beauty of having two masts. The sails are smaller. In fact, I think Kent sails it by himself,' he says, referring to the professional skipper he employs to look after his fleet of yachts scattered around the globe. I must have looked sceptical as he gives this some thought before going on. 'Look, I'll tell you what I'll do. Kent can come over to the US to re-commission the boat with you and get you started. He knows the boat well, and it may take a bit of work to get her going after such a long layoff. I'll also lend you Randel for a while to help.'

It turns out Randel is another employee of Tim's. He's from St Lucia and Tim met him there several years ago after sailing El Oro across the Atlantic as part of the ARC rally. I shake my head slightly bemused. I had no idea he had all these people working for him supporting his sailing habit. It should have given me a clue it's not easy to manage these sorts of boats short-handed.

I mention the idea is exciting and we're keen but it's also a little daunting.

'Oh, I'm sure there'll be challenges,' he says, eyes sparkling. 'But it beats commuting any day.'

From my side it's hard to argue with that logic. I've been working for the same business for twenty-four years, and although I've had a good career with them, the truth is I'm bored and stuck in a rut. There was an opportunity for change a couple of years earlier and I secured a role managing the business's export sales into Europe. The role was based in the region, and I briefly moved to London ahead of Til in January 2020. A few weeks later the world tumbled into chaos, the pandemic sweeping across the globe, and I retreated to Australia, fortunate to get one of the last flights out of London just as our possessions headed off in a shipping container the other way. Since getting back, I've been working from home managing the business from our place in Taralga in country NSW, keeping antisocial hours on the phone to European distributors late into the night. I am tired of this and very much ready for a change.

Til on the other hand has a career heading on an upward trajectory. She's an artist, working out of our back room which is converted to a studio. She likes to paint abstract landscapes capturing the essence of the Australian bush in a series of green and ochre tones. She also paints lots of other subjects and has a lucrative sideline in dog portraits. Covid saw her business take off from a modest enterprise selling the occasional painting to being unable to keep up with demand. People were stuck at home, bored, staring at their blank walls and the orders for paintings flew in. She sells through a few galleries mainly in NSW but when an up-and-coming gallery in Melbourne take her into their stable, things accelerate and she's able to edge her prices up. We're both worried taking a year out will bring this momentum to a halt. 'Do you think it'll be possible to paint on the boat?' she wonders. We don't know the answer although it doesn't seem likely she'll be able to paint in oils. They take a couple of weeks to dry and wet paint on a moving boat isn't going to work.

I exchange a few emails with Tim. His are full of encouragement and he recommends we start by heading to the Caribbean for a few months. 'Warm steady breezes. Just the thing for getting to know the boat before you head further afield.' He suggests we make St Lucia our base as we can get some work done on the boat there. He and Kent have used some of the tradesmen there before. Rodney Bay at the northern tip of the island is a fabulous safe harbour where we can rendezvous with guests. St Lucia is also Randel's home, he comes from Soufriere, in the south of the island, so we'd be delivering him home as well. When I express some concerns about the length of the ocean crossing from the north-eastern US coast, he tells me Kent can skipper the boat as far as the islands. When we get there, he'll hand over to us. Nothing seems to be much of a problem for Tim and his emails are usually signed off with encouraging epithets like, 'Don't rush. Life is not a rehearsal.'

I have some questions for him around who pays for what if things break on the boat. My experience of boats is things break all the time and on a large yacht like El Oro they'll be expensive to fix. 'Get in touch with Kent to work out the arrangements,' he tells me. 'If you have problems with the boat don't bring them to me; I'll only defer to Kent anyway. I want to get the odd postcard hearing about the good times you're having.'

As instructed, I give Kent a ring. He must have been briefed by Tim as he's expecting my call and is enthusiastic about the proposed arrangement. We discuss how the finances will work. The upshot is Tim will pay whatever commissioning costs are necessary to get the boat up and running and leave us with a full tank of fuel. Like a hire car, we need to leave the tank full when we return it. The diesel tank is 2,000L so hopefully we don't need to fill up too often. With breakages the agreement seems a bit vague. We will pay for anything we, or our guests, break through carelessness or negligence, but if something breaks or fails that would likely have broken anyway, we should send the bill to Kent and Tim will pick up the cost. This sounds simple, but how easy will it be to implement in practice?

The timings are also a bit vague. Kent tells me El Oro is sitting, chocked up somewhere called Safe Harbor, Wickford

Cove. I search up the address on Google Maps and I find what can only be her. A fenced off space, behind a large shed set back from the water, is packed with boats. Towards the back, there's a prominent elliptical shape, twice the size of any of the other vessels packed in tightly around her. There's no way she can be reached until most of the neighbouring boats have been launched, by which time it will be early summer. Tim and Kent are sailing in the Mediterranean from April through until July so Kent can't get to the US to help us launch until after he's finished in Europe, and he's put Tim's other boat away for the winter. We discuss meeting in Rhode Island late August which later slips to mid-September. This gives us around six months to think about the trip. It's a surreal time. We don't hear much from Tim in the interim and I catch myself wondering if the thing is really going to happen. Is it a figment of my imagination, an idea thrown up but cast aside? It seems so unlikely someone would lend us a yacht, without even knowing much about our sailing abilities.

There's plenty of things we should be doing to pack up our lives, but we're overtaken by inertia and don't do anything. I'm reluctant to break the news to work that I'm leaving in case the trip doesn't happen. It seems crazy to sacrifice a good job of 24 years for the promise of a voyage that might not eventuate. We want to recruit friends to come and join us, but it's hard to convince people to commit when we're not certain ourselves the voyage will take place.

I'm still prevaricating over telling my boss my plans when he calls to say the business is restructuring, and would I be interested in taking a redundancy? *Would I – really?* I have some trouble stifling the whoop of excitement as I tell him that sounds like a sensible idea. This changes the game altogether and financially takes the pressure off. Now all we need is to hear from Tim.

A few weeks later he sends us a link to a recording of Cavafy's poem, Ithaca. 'Don't rush the journey,' he tells us.

When you set out on your journey to Ithaca,
pray that the road is long,
full of adventure, full of knowledge.
The Lestrygonians and the Cyclops,
the angry Poseidon - do not fear them:
You will never find such as these on your path,
if your thoughts remain lofty, if a fine
emotion touches your spirit and your body.
The Lestrygonians and the Cyclops,
the fierce Poseidon you will never encounter,
if you do not carry them within your soul,
if your soul does not set them up before you.

Pray that the road is long.
That the summer mornings are many, when,
with such pleasure, with such joy
you will enter ports seen for the first time;
stop at Phoenician markets,
and purchase fine merchandise,
mother-of-pearl and coral, amber and ebony,
and sensual perfumes of all kinds,
as many sensual perfumes as you can;
visit many Egyptian cities,
to learn and learn from scholars.

Always keep Ithaca in your mind.
To arrive there is your ultimate goal.
But do not hurry the voyage at all.
It is better to let it last for many years;
and to anchor at the island when you are old,

rich with all you have gained on the way,
not expecting that Ithaca will offer you riches.

Ithaca has given you the beautiful voyage.
Without her you would have never set out on the road.
She has nothing more to give you.

And if you find her poor, Ithaca has not deceived you.
Wise as you have become, with so much experience,
you must already have understood what Ithaca means.

It seems we're going.

SEPTEMBER

It's a long way from my mother's house in West Mersea to Boston via London and Reykjavik and it's late in the evening when we get there. We leave Mersea early in the morning to avoid the crowds heading into London for the Queen's lying-in-state. Radio bulletins describing thousands of people pouring into the capital initially seem alarmist until we grind to a halt in the world's biggest traffic jam somewhere near Elephant and Castle. Thinking we're being clever we turn off the main road and accidentally stumble into the pricey congestion zone. Eventually, with little time to spare, we get the car back to the rental office and wrestle our heavy bags to Victoria and onto the Gatwick Express in time to catch our flight.

Many hours later in Boston airport, minds in neutral, we're queueing for immigration when I see Til rummaging in her handbag. The searching becomes more frantic, and she looks at me with anguish; her passport is still in the seat pocket on the plane. 'Are you sure?' I ask. She nods, and we push our way out of the concertinaed queue, running back along the endless passageway to the distant gate. It's hard to find when you go in reverse, but we get there after some searching, to discover the gate is closed and deserted. There is no one around to ask for help. The plane is still there, we can see it through the narrow, slit window and there are people moving inside, but we can't attract their attention. We wave and thump on the window but to no avail. The doors to the gate are closed with a large red sign: 'Do not open. Doors alarmed.' We glance at each other and in unspoken agreement, push on the metal bar running across the threshold and the doors swing open. We don't get far. As advertised, there's an ear-splitting alarm and we're not yet at the boarding ramp when swarms of security guards appear from nowhere. It's as if we've stamped on an ant's nest; one moment the place is deserted, the next there's a swarm of state troopers rushing towards us. They don't pull a weapon, but twitchy hands hover near holsters ready to draw if we cause any trouble. 'I'm so sorry, it's my passport, I left it in seat 35A' says Til, hands in the air, and we stand in silence waiting uneasily while someone is despatched to collect it.

To our relief it's produced but we're not allowed to go until we've been thoroughly processed. After a stern telling-off, a policeman takes our details and there's a long wait while they're relayed to someone on the end of a phone who checks them out. Eventually, we get the all-clear and, not trusted to make our own way to immigration, are escorted back to where we started by a Massachusetts state trooper with very shiny boots and a large gun.

Unfortunately, in the interim, more planes have arrived, and the queue is now horrendous. An hour later we get through to find the baggage carousel for our flight has long closed with no sign of our bags. No-one seems able to help and everyone from Icelandair has gone home for the night, so we give up on our luggage and grab a cab to our Airbnb in Roxbury, a little way out of town. For some reason we haven't received entry instructions and for a while can't get onto the host, so we sit on the doorstep at 11.00pm. Perhaps we can camp on the veranda. Eventually we sort this out and collapse into bed. Hopefully the rest of our stay in the US will be less exhausting.

Next morning, we catch the train back to the airport to re-unite with our bags before heading into town to check out Boston, ending up in the Museum of Fine Arts. We walk several miles back to our lodgings admiring the distinctive architecture; row upon row of timber weatherboard houses often three or more stories high. To our Australian eyes these seem something of a fire risk. On every street corner we're greeted with a friendly 'good afternoon.' It's very different from London or even Sydney where strangers don't speak to each other. Back at our lodgings we try and cook some dinner but in the kitchen there's not a single pot, or even a kettle. There's only the drip coffee machine.

We walk back into town the next day for more exploring – we're getting our daily steps up. In a park near the city centre, we briefly tag onto a tour led by a man dressed up as an eighteenth-century New Englander. He's enthralling his followers, waving his arms in the air whilst telling the story of the dastardly British redcoats and the Boston massacre. It's impossible to miss that Boston is the birthplace of the American Revolution and everywhere there are reminders: street names, squares, statues and monuments. We take the train out to Harvard to see their art museum and admire the beautifully manicured lawns and immaculate buildings. The museum itself has a vast collection of Monets, there seem to be more in America than in France. It's an incredible collection and there are also works by most major European and American artists. On the way out we pass an art supply shop where, inspired by what we've seen, Til stocks up on painting materials.

The next day we wrestle with our bags again - taking the train to Providence, a delightful city we'll later come to know well, and from there into a hire car and on to North Kingston where we have another room booked. This one is an overpriced, dark space under someone's house. The listing on Airbnb shows the nice view from the doorway out onto a lake – but for some reason fails to make any mention of the route 4 motorway a few feet away. The roar of traffic is constant and a bit overwhelming. Nevertheless, Joy our host, is friendly and gives us fresh eggs from her chickens to welcome us into the troglodytic space.

It's only a mile or so from the marina in Wickford Cove so we take the opportunity to go and have a first look at El Oro. Safe Harbor turns out to be a brand name, it's a chain of marinas operating all over the US. The one at Wickford is relatively small and at the head of an attractive cove off the Narraganset. It's early autumn and most boats are still in the water, so the hardstand is almost empty. We can't miss El Oro; out of the water she seems huge. Shrink-wrapped in white plastic sheeting and supported by aluminium props, she is standing on her keel, towering above us as we walk underneath her. She's by far the largest boat in the yard.

Kent pushes back his arrival a few days and as we can't get going without him, we have some time to kill. We drive over to Newport to check out the famous Mansions. We follow the cliff walk winding around the southern headlands beneath some of the imposing dwellings established by outrageously wealthy 19th century industrialists, and afterwards we amble into town to have a look at the end of season sales on wet weather gear. We make a mess of the Helly Hansen store, trying on every item in the sale rack. Til's brother connects us with some friends of his, Willy and Lowie, who live in a fabulous house above a pub on the main street in Newport. They are building a roof terrace, and we sit up there amongst the builders' detritus looking out over the famous harbour, enjoying a drink as the evening light turns golden over the moored boats.

After a couple of days, Kent arrives, driving a car he's borrowed from a friend in New Hampshire. He's tall, sixtyish and fit looking with a shock of grey hair and an air of confidence. A New Zealander living in Aosta in the mountains of northern Italy, he's worked for Tim for almost 20 years starting out as chef on board one of his yachts and later becoming the skipper. He splits his time between skiing in the off season and sailing Tim's various yachts. I mention it sounds like an idyllic lifestyle, and he agrees, but admits the lifestyle plays havoc with his personal life. He's away from home a lot and doesn't get to see his kids as often as he'd like.

The next afternoon Randel follows, flying in from St Lucia. In contrast with Kent, he's taciturn and reserved, although with a ready smile. He's also a lot younger, in his early thirties. He has left two small children at home and regularly has them on Facetime chatting with him as he works on the boat. The marina manager, a gigantic bear of a man called Larry, is adamant we're not permitted to stay on board whilst the yacht is on the hardstand, so Kent and Randel take lodgings in nearby Greenwich.

Together, we clear the plastic away from the boat and it becomes obvious it's going to take a bit more than a quick antifoul to get the boat in the water. Three years out of the water has taken a toll. There's a green tinge to the teak deck which can be scrubbed clean, but it takes a lot longer for the musty smell below to dissipate.

The saloon on El Oro is a magnificent space. It's as wide and comfortable as a small apartment. The interior is lined with varnished timber and the craftmanship is exquisite. Heavy laminated mahogany frames disappear into delicate timber panelling. Above the worn leather seating there are rows of books which make the place cosy and homely. In pride of place in front of the two portholes, there's a crystal decanter secured to the hull by a wooden collar. 'That,' says Kent, 'is something you'll need to take good care of. It's Lord Nelson's decanter.' The decanter was given to Tim by a grateful patient; a perfect gift for someone who has spent a lifetime loving the sea and admiring seafaring adventurers like Cook, Cochrane and Nelson.

Behind the saloon is the galley. It's more of a typical boat kitchen; a narrow space with a gimbaled stove. There's plenty of working surface which is great when the boat's flat, as well as a full-size fridge and a microwave. Til sorts through the various drawers and lockers and pulls out two different sized pressure cookers. 'These look scary,' she says, putting them away again.

There are three separate cabins in front of the saloon, each with two bunks and in the bow section there is a more traditional vee berth with a double mattress. Going the other way, towards the stern, there's a corridor leading aft from the saloon, lined on one side with drawers full of tools and a cupboard for wet weather gear. On the other side there's a low door to the engine room, an airless space beneath the cockpit with metal floorboards. The two main engines are crammed into this tight space along with a generator and all the associated fuel lines, filters and electric cabling. Rainwater has found its way in and all the exposed metal is covered in an orange layer of corrosion. Past the engine room and at the end of the corridor is the owner's cabin at the back of the boat where we'll sleep. It's not very marital, there are two separate bunks, one on each side of the cabin, both under a row of books.

Surprisingly the house batteries still have some charge and after a bit of coaxing are revived. The engine batteries must be replaced, and Kent locks himself in the engine room for days cleaning up the rust and playing with the corroded electrics until eventually he can turn the engines over. To my untrained eye, the electrics seem complicated. There are 12V batteries for starting the engines and running some outlets. The house batteries are 24V and run most of the systems. An inverter supplies 240V outlets which power the freshwater pump, fridge freezer and coffee machine – distressingly that's out of action – as well as the very cool multi adapter plug sockets accepting almost any plug on the planet. Shore power comes in at 110V as we're in America and there are a few locally purchased appliances such as the vacuum cleaner that can only be run on this. The wiring is a bird's nest of cables and very hard to follow. Kent comments this was done in the yard in Burma. He follows up wryly, 'the Burmese are very good with wood…'

The deck of El Oro is five metres above the hardstand and to climb aboard we scale a ladder the yard has lent us. Kent lashes it to the rail so it's secure, but it's still disconcerting looking at the concrete beneath us as we make our way aboard. Til and I are armed with spray bottles of vinegar and a cloth and set to cleaning the boat from top to bottom: emptying lockers of damp clothes left behind when the boat was put away three years ago. Our days are spent sorting, re-stowing and organising. We manage to fix the coffee machine. It seems it needs re-priming after being left unattended for so long and we're able to take off the side panels and inject water into the tiny pump and it springs into life delivering perfect espressos.

After a week, we move out of our troglodyte hole and into what might be the smallest Airbnb in the world. Called the

Radio Shack (it was once someone's Grandfather's ham radio shed), it is a single room slightly larger than a double bed with a tiny kitchen. At least this one has a few pots and pans. There is also a cupboard doubling as a bathroom. All of which sets us back $150 a night. Four nights of this is enough and we move up the road to East Greenwich to bunk in with Kent and Randel. They are sharing a room in some lodgings run by a young Syrian guy called Elias who charges us $60 per night cash which seems a bit more reasonable. It's an old, traditional American house with three floors, lots of bedrooms and a shared kitchen and bathroom. Elias himself moves around and seems to sleep wherever a room is vacant. If there isn't a room free, he sleeps in the corridor between Kent and Randel's room and the kitchen. Elias has taken on the American dream with enthusiasm. He works full-time as an engineer as well as managing his two rental properties. As a hobby he is studying watchmaking. 'I might be able to do repairs as a sideline,' he tells me with a smile. He produces a machine which he hooks up to my watch. 'That's not bad,' he says. 'Your watch is gaining seven seconds a day.'

OCTOBER

THE DAYS DRAG ON as there are more and more jobs to complete before we can launch. We scrape, fill and antifoul the hull; we remove the hot water system which isn't working and take it apart. Randel and I put it back together again and mysteriously it seems to produce hot water once more. We re-plumb the gas bottles which are sealed in the lazarette, a deep locker at the back of the boat used to contain all manner of miscellaneous items. We clean up and epoxy a rotten cockpit hatch cover. We prime and paint different coloured sections on the anchor chain to mark the depth. We discover where the water has been getting into the engine room and Kent digs out a band of rot which stretches over a meter around the cockpit floor before sealing this back up with epoxy. The yard has told us there's no room to stay in the marina once we launch, so we're keen to get as much as possible done while we're ashore and have easy access to shops and facilities.

Whilst all this is happening, we also take some time to explore our surroundings. It's now early October, the weather is getting cooler, and the trees are turning shades of gold, amber and deep red. We make several visits to nearby Providence, the capital of Rhode Island. It's a university city and has a relaxed, friendly vibe. Through mutual friends we meet Sarah who grew up in the area and she shows us around and introduces us to some of the local bars and cafes.

Another day we drive out to New Bedford in the pouring rain and visit that historic old town. The woman in the visitor centre is chatty and when she hears we're from Australia she tells us we should read up about the Catalpa – a ship from New Bedford despatched to undertake a daring rescue of some Irish convicts in Freemantle in the late 1800s. We go to the whaling museum before climbing back in the car and driving to Cape Cod for a look. It's a bit further than we anticipated and it's dusk when we get there with the rain still pounding against the windscreen. The ocean beach is cold and deserted with alarming signs warning of Great White Sharks. It's not tempting to swim. We take a quick look around the town which is full of cute cafes as well as a lot of leather, and rainbow flags. It's dark as we head back on the long drive to East Greenwich, stopping off at Dunkin' for a donut… perhaps not our smartest move.

The following Sunday we go the other way to Connecticut, heading to Yale - which also has some great art collections. After all, we'd already been to see Harvard. On the way we detour via Mystic, a beautiful New England port with some interesting square riggers tied up against the wharf. We leave the Seaport Museum, advertised as the nation's leading maritime museum, for another day. From there we go on to New Haven and the art museums which if anything, are more impressive than the ones in Boston.

After ten days in Elias's place, Kent and Randel are moved upstairs as he has another booking. A young couple and another friend going to a wedding of an old fraternity buddy are now sharing our space. One of them is a US Marine and arrives dressed in full ceremonial regalia, an array of medals on his chest. We get chatting and I mention years ago I did a short service commission in the British Army. 'Thank you for your service,' says the marine's girlfriend oblivious to the fact my service was for a different country. There are pre-wedding drinks the first night and they partake of these enthusiastically. The couple comes back first around 1.30am and after stumbling around and having a short row go quiet. We, but apparently not they, are woken some hours later by loud banging on the walls from their mate who is annoyed he's been left behind and hasn't been given the door code. A moment later he's in the house having broken in through the bathroom window and loudly berates his friends for abandoning him. We can hear everything through the paper-thin walls, but his mates are out for the count and there's no response.

Another week goes by – with two steps forward and one back. We find the cockpit still leaking despite the repair to the rotted area, so that takes more work. We re-install the water heater only to take it out again when we discover it's still leaking. There's better news with the engines. After a lot of work on the electrics, Kent finally gets them to fire, although the generator is now giving trouble. It has multiple sensors preventing it from starting if there's even a hint of something wrong. There's only room for one in the engine room and it's a little frustrating I can't see what Kent's doing, as I know in future it will be me having to coax these engines into life. When I ask him to show me what he's working on, he demurs, saying we'll have plenty of time to go through this later.

We spend a day removing the 600 litres of old diesel from the tanks – first pumping back and forth from one tank to the other to try and stir up the sediment before running it over the side to some 50-gallon fuel drums provided by the yard. There are eight fuel tanks, and we go to some lengths to avoid spilling diesel, so the process takes a long time. We work on the freshwater systems and get the pump back into action. Plugging the through hull outlet from the galley sink with a pipe to a bucket we now have running water on board. All small steps forward.

We have another change of guests in the boarding house – this time a Korean family come up from New Jersey to go fishing. Elias sleeps on the sofa in the living room as they take his corridor spot. There are about 10 of them– it's not clear how they fit in the room, but they are quiet and courteous in comparison with the wedding party the previous weekend. The kids are young and seem slightly embarrassed by their parents. They tell us they found the fishing boring and at dinner they eat the vegetables and not the fish. They remind us of our children.

Eventually there's good news, the yard now has a space in the marina, so Kent is comfortable we can launch El Oro. The process is smooth as the yard team swing into action. The huge travel lift is manoeuvred to the yacht and 40 tonnes of boat are soon swaying gently in the slings. Randel slaps some antifoul on the patches we couldn't reach when the yacht was sitting on its props and we trundle slowly to the onshore fuel dock where we take on 2,000L of diesel. It takes a while to fill up. From there the travel lift rolls at walking pace to the dock where the boat is lowered gently into the water.

❁

Sleeping on the boat is much more comfortable than Elias's boarding house. We have an ensuite head with shower with hot water. It's very different from any yacht I've sailed on before. The nights are now cold, so we have a small portable heater in our cabin and it's a snug hideaway. The beautiful autumn weather has gone – replaced with wet misty, raining conditions so we're mainly working on inside jobs for now. There are still some issues preventing us from leaving – a seized alternator being the main one, but also lots of teething issues with the generator and the multiple sensors controlling it.

Our friend RL arrives from Sydney after spending a few days with his brother in New York. I've sailed a lot with RL over the years, both cruising and racing and he's someone I trust offshore. On land he's a law unto himself, but that's a different story. He introduces a new energy into the group and is full of enthusiasm, pushing for solutions and raring to get going. This irritates Kent, who points out to him we've been working on the boat for nearly six weeks, and we'll be ready when we're ready.

It's not all work, we also make time to enjoy ourselves. One rainy day we have some visitors for lunch. Doc Greenaway and his wife Heather are old friends of Tim and Kent: Australians who now live in the US. Doc is also a legendary sailor who sailed in some of the early Australian America's cup campaigns in the sixties and seventies. Over a bottle of wine or two he regales us with stories from those days.

Now we're getting close to a departure date, we're joined by a friend of Kent's who is going to accompany us for the crossing to the Caribbean. In his late 50's, Jeff is short, smiley and has long, flowing golden locks he has a habit of flicking from side to side as if in a shampoo advert. He's a great storyteller and has a disarming knack of telling amusing tales against himself. He seems to have had a life lurching from one near disaster to another and there are plenty of stories. Kent tells us they met Jeff in Tonga when Kent was skippering Cordelia, one of Tim's earlier yachts. At the time, Jeff had a kayak with a small sail and was trying to make his way through some of the Pacific Islands when he got into trouble off Nuku'alofa. He misjudged the current and his kayak was picked up and dumped onto a coral reef. Kent and the crew of Cordelia were at a function at the Australian High Commission when Jeff was bought in by his rescuer wet and bedraggled. The High Commissioner's reaction was apparently to exclaim, 'Someone get that man a beer!'

Kurt, the rigger, turns up with a colleague to check over the standing rigging and to string some additional halyards. The two of them spend some time setting up the running backstays which are led from high on the mast, down via gigantic and expensive looking pulley blocks and into a huge clutch bolted to the deck. Kent informs us these clutches cost the same as a small car so we should take good care of them! The windward runner must be clamped up tight while the leeward one is released and taken forward during each tack. We are later to become intimately acquainted with these lines. Kurt is about to pack up and go when his colleague notices some rust at the top of one of the mizzen cap shrouds.

'Um… when did you say you wanted to set off...?' he says, scratching at the rust with a screwdriver.

Our spirits sink as another delay is introduced. They need to order replacements and won't be able to get them for another week. Will we ever leave this marina?

Morale is improved by bending on the mainsail. We slide in battens to a beautiful and nearly new grey carbon fibre sail and wrestle the cars into the track on the mast. It all looks horribly expensive. I make a mental note to myself not to break anything.

Sunday 30th dawns cold and clear. There's a layer of frost on the deck and heading to the marina amenities is a hazardous exercise. We take a break from the boat as the surveyor is coming back to finish poking around and Kent offers to run us across to Mystic. It's a perfect autumn day – warm in the sun, but there's a bite to the air; you want your jacket on.

The Mystic Seaport Maritime Museum is a bit like Disneyland for boats. It's a rambling collection of exhibits and attractions spread out across a re-created 19th century maritime village. Some buildings house exhibitions, or demonstrations of activities like cooperage or sail making, whilst others house whale boats and assorted paraphernalia. In season it would be crowded with tourists, now it's deserted; we have the place to ourselves. Alongside the wharves are various square riggers including the Joseph Conrad. This was a small ship owned by Australian Alan Villiers who sailed around the world in the 1930s with an amateur crew. I have his book at home so it's fascinating to see the vessel itself. It's missing some spars and is a little tired – but she's reassuringly sturdy and has pleasing workmanlike lines. With a few like-minded friends we could give her a lick of paint and she'd be ready to go to sea. A little further on is the last remaining wooden whaler in the US, the Charles W. Morgan, which has been fully restored and is now a seagoing vessel again. We're able to wander all over these ships, and others, and there's usually a white bearded enthusiast on board keen to explain all the details such as how the trypots worked and how the valuable oil was collected.

There is the replica of the Amistad, a Spanish slave ship taken over in an uprising by African slaves in 1839. The mutineers spare the lives of two Spanish navigators on the condition they direct the ship back to their home. During the voyage however the Spanish gradually turn the ship north and bring it to port in Long Island where the Africans are promptly arrested as runaway slaves. Initially condemned to be sent to Cuba where they were originally bound for, a group of abolitionists take up their cause and a long and complex legal battle ensues. After three years the Supreme Court rules they've been illegally kidnapped and eventually the surviving Africans are returned to Sierra Leone.

In the afternoon we find a restaurant on the river and deciding we've done enough touristing, we settle in for a long and well lubricated lunch.

NOVEMBER

THE MONTH STARTS with more last-minute jobs; we make multiple trips to the marine consignment store in Newport, a treasure trove of nautical craziness. More mundanely we also frequent Home Depot and West Marine looking for epoxy or a new grease gun. We retrieve our life raft from the service centre outside Newport, marvelling at that successful business. They seem to have a monopoly for the region and there are dozens of life rafts stacked up outside waiting to be serviced. It must be a licence to print money.

El Oro is missing a tender, so we purchase a dinghy from Larry in the yard. It's an inflatable with a fibreglass bottom previously belonging to some guy from South Carolina who hasn't paid his storage fees. Kent is enthusiastic about the 20hp Yamaha outboard: El Oro has no bow thruster, so we can use the outboard to push us into and out of tight spaces. Unfortunately, it proves hard to get started and we play with it for hours, coaxing it into life. Eventually it fires, but runs unevenly, a forerunner of challenges to come.

We're close to being ready to go but the final to-do list keeps growing. We have a couple more days' work planned when suddenly, almost without warning, we're off. Larry has become impatient with us, looking to free up space in the marina, now busy with boats being taken out of the water. 'You've overstayed your welcome – it's time to move out' he growls. He has let us stay for free in the marina since launching almost two weeks earlier, so he has a point. There's a pile of unstowed equipment on deck but regardless we untie the lines and ease off the dock in the late afternoon sunshine.

It's exciting to head through the channel, packed with moored boats, and out past the breakwater for the first time. We coil up the mooring lines as we motor past the red and green channel markers and El Oro glides into the wide expanse of Narragansett Bay. Except for the occasional fishing vessel, we have the place to ourselves. A watery sun sets behind the western shore, and we scramble to put some more clothes on as the warmth of the day turns quickly to an evening chill. Halfway across to Jamestown Island in the gathering dusk one engine splutters to a halt. A minute later the other one follows suit and we're drifting in silence.

'Go forward and drop the anchor.' Kent takes control of the situation and soon we have 30m of chain out in 7m of water. It seems there is air in the fuel lines, so he bleeds the engines and after some messing around we are back in action. We hoist the staysail and reefed main and retrieve the anchor. Rounding the northern end of Jamestown Island, where magnificent gardens run to the water, we harden up onto the wind to beat up the eastern channel in the dark. With the ebbing tide under us we make good progress, and our third tack brings us under the Newport bridge and past Rose Island on our port side. Unlit buoys loom out of the darkness as we glide past, and we ease sheets to round Fort Adams before dropping anchor off the Ida Lewis yacht club.

Waking up in a new anchorage when you have arrived in the dark is always special. The mysterious shapes and dark spaces so cautiously negotiated are laid bare and the setting never looks quite as you imagined. This morning is mirror calm and the sun is trying to shine through the mist which is obscuring the bridge and much of the Newport foreshore, although on the slope back from the beach we can make out the famous New York Yacht Club. There is one other anchored yacht, a catamaran which leaves early and a handful of moored yachts amid the multitude of empty mooring buoys. We're well out of season.

After a slow morning we take a berth at the low-key Newport Yacht Club, very different from the much swankier New York Yacht Club across the bay. Kent heads off in the car to the Big Apple to pick up his girlfriend Colleen from the airport and we go ashore to hunt for some last-minute supplies including new sparkplugs for the troublesome outboard and 'cheap' engine oil from Walmart. Later that evening, we're joined by Jay, a friend of Kent's from New Hampshire who will sail with us as far as New York. Til tries the pressure cooker and we're all amazed to see a whole chicken cooked in just twenty minutes. What's more it's juicy and delicious. This will be a game changer when we're offshore. RL, who's always dangerous on land, leads a shore party into town and we have too many beers before returning with two gigantic pumpkins which have previously done duty as a Halloween display. Randel jokes about starting a pumpkin farm on the hills of St Lucia.

We're a bit slow the next morning, some of us nursing sore

heads as we sort through the last of the chaos on deck from our rushed departure from Wickford and lash Randel's pumpkins to the stern rail. Colleen who came in very late the previous night, appears from one of the cabins. She's Scottish, but lives in Chamonix where she works as a sports masseur. Her real passion is climbing, something she's obviously very good at, as she's sponsored by several different businesses. She's chatty and bubbly and adds a breath of fresh air to the group.

The last-minute shopping expeditions never seems to end, and more things keep appearing on the list, but eventually enough's enough. After paying the $73 marina fee, the cheapest berthage we'll get for a very long time, we cast off. We tow the dinghy through the East Passage before hoisting it onto the davits in the shelter behind Beavertail Point. This is an exercise we'll get very good at in the coming months. Continuing south we leave Narragansett Bay, turning west at Point Judith following the setting sun and hoist the staysail and mizzen while leaving the engines running. Given the problems we had coming out of Wickford we're keen to give them a decent run; we need to be able to trust them before heading into the fast-flowing current of the East River in New York.

Leaving the Narragansett, the boat lifts and falls to the Atlantic swell before the water gradually flattens off again as we head into Long Island Sound. With a knot and a half of favourable current we're doing 10 knots over the ground and Block Island appears and soon after fades behind us in the evening gloom. Motor sailing hard on the wind we make rapid progress towards Fisher Island, our destination for the night. Avoiding the myriad of shoals on the eastern approach to the island we track parallel with the shoreline until we come to the flashing red beacon marking rocks off the western tip. Disconnecting the autopilot to bear away around the island, Kent spins the wheel, but the boat doesn't turn. There's no steering. The strong current, which should be sweeping us away from the land and into deep water, eddies around the point and carries us back towards the rocks.

'Get the emergency tiller from the lazarette' is the order and we scrabble to retrieve the heavy wooden lever as the boat drifts out of control in the darkness towards the rocky coast. Fixing it to the steering post we are unable to move the rudder; we also need to disconnect the hydraulic system via a lever at the bottom of the lazarette. Everything that was on deck at Wickford has been stowed in this locker along with hundreds of metres of rope and various other pieces of equipment that haven't found a home elsewhere. It all comes out onto the deck with an urgency driven by the sound of breaking waves somewhere in front of us. There's a tense silence from the skipper but eventually the release valve is located, and the tiller is free, and we turn away from the coast. The tiller faces backwards, towards the stern of the boat, so it turns the opposite way to a normal tiller which takes a bit of getting used to. It works effectively, and with the help of the GPS plotter we make our way around to a sheltered cove on the north of the island. The nervous tension is not done with as we lose an engine on the way around, but fortunately our second engine continues to throb steadily and a few minutes later there's a rumble of chain through the hawser pipe and the anchor drops to the bottom.

The need to catch the tide at 5.00am the next morning has us up early. Kent diagnoses our steering problems as a lack of hydraulic fluid – perhaps something to do with using the autohelm. The run from Newport was the first time we'd used the autopilot. The system works harder than manual steering, constantly making corrections, each time pumping hydraulic fluid through the lines. We're not sure if there's a leak, we can't see any excess fluid anywhere so maybe there was air in the system. We top up the fluid and the problem appears to be solved. The engine cutting out is a bit more concerning. It's resolved by bleeding once again but we're not sure why we're getting this air in the fuel lines. Kent theorizes it's something to do with the pump being too powerful and aerating the fuel, but we're not sure. One thing is for certain, we want to be able to rely on our engines when we're in a tight space. We motor sail again despite a decent breeze to give the engines another good test.

All day we head westwards through Long Island Sound. The day is cool and overcast and the scenery is all watery shades of grey. Sheltered water and a favourable tide mean we make good progress in the morning averaging around 10 knots over the ground. At midday the current turns against us and the wind drops cutting our speed in half. We're still experiencing engine problems and every hour or so the engines splutter to a halt and need bleeding before they can be restarted.

The low coastline gradually comes closer on both sides as the sound narrows. Mostly featureless, it is punctuated by the occasional isolated chimney from some industrial complex that seem to take forever to move past as we inch against the current. Although it's a weekend there are few boats out on the water in the autumn chill. As evening falls the sun breaks through and, in the distance, we get a first glimpse of the Manhattan skyline. There's a rush to get cameras with the expectation of a spectacular sunset behind the skyscrapers but the buildings recede into a band of smog and the sun is gone.

The next morning is unseasonably warm with bright sunshine and no hint of haze. We sit at anchor in Manhasset Bay, drinking coffee, waiting for the optimal time to transit the East River. The current runs as fast as 5 knots and we want to go through as close to slack water as possible. A brisk northerly breeze has sprung up and there's a tangy smell of dirty river water as we push off and follow the channel through the city. Initially wide, the river narrows as we head under the flightpath for LaGuardia airport and past the Rikers Island prison and its overflow, the grim looking prison barge moored on the other side. Reputedly the prison barge is closed, but we can see people playing basketball on the top deck, behind razor wire, so we're not sure. It's reminiscent of the prison hulks that lined the Thames in Dickensian times. The strong breeze has delayed us slightly and we have more current with us than anticipated; it sweeps us ever faster through the narrowing channel. Tugs pushing loaded barges head up and down the river. Hugely powerful they seem to navigate the strong currents and crosswind with little difficulty, but we give them a wide berth. We sweep past Randall's Island and Hell Gate and into the narrows. Familiar landmarks come and go – the Empire State Building, the Chrysler building; the cityscape changing to towers of glass and steel as we pass the financial district. City workers taking their lunch break in the autumn sunshine glance up as we pass by. A few minutes later we're under the Brooklyn bridge and into the tide race at the southern tip of Manhattan.

We motor towards the magnificent and surprisingly large Statue of Liberty standing proud above the grey choppy water. Thousands of migrants have passed here seeking a better life and it's a potent symbol embodying hope and opportunity. We take the opportunity to pick up new crew. We lower the dinghy and Randel runs Jay and Colleen ashore. Jay is leaving us to make his way home to New Hampshire and Colleen is going to the hairdresser and taking a few days off the boat. Randel brings back our new crewmember, Thomas, who has flown in that morning from Stockholm. A good friend of Tim and Kent, he has sailed extensively on El Oro crossing the Atlantic with them as well as sailing from Antigua to Bermuda. Thomas has a reassuring air of competence which we appreciate as darkness falls and we prepare to head offshore. We bring the dinghy back on board in the shelter of Sandy Hook and head out to sea tracking parallel with the New Jersey coast. We're aiming for the Delaware River, a hundred miles to our south. In the Atlantic, tropical storm Nicole is brewing and looks like it may head up the east coast, so we want to make sure we're in good shelter.

Our first overnight sail is challenging. The breeze builds from astern to around 25 knots with a short breaking chop in the shallow water. We hoist the main, mizzen and staysail and for a while make good progress to the south surging through the building seaway. Without any warning we have a repeat of the steering problems. The boat is on autopilot when it rounds up into the wind out of control. The sails flog as we rush once more to connect the emergency tiller. We hand steer for a while whilst refilling the hydraulics, after which the wheel is operational again.

Later, I'm on watch with RL with reduced sail – this time staysail and mizzen as well as one engine ticking over. We're still doing 7 knots and making good progress south, the orange loom of New York fading behind us. We have been watching two fishing boats on AIS which have been largely stationary but are heading towards us. We have the autohelm on and are discussing the best way to avoid them when the steering goes again. This time we have no control in the strong wind and are unable to prevent the gybe – the mizzen boom crashing over out of control breaking the sheet block and pulling the boom gooseneck out of the mast. With a struggle we get the steering stabilised and the mizzen lowered and lashed and go through the process again of refilling the hydraulics. It seems the autopilot is the problem – there must be a leak in the system somewhere, but we'll need to wait until calmer waters to check.

The rest of the night is less eventful and by dawn we are off Atlantic City. A series of scattered high-rise buildings stand stark against the low shoreline in the clear morning light. It's bitterly cold and we're rugged up in multiple layers. The wind is still strong – force 5-6 and is pushing up a short steep chop with foaming crests on all sides. El Oro pushes through these with little trouble – the occasional toppling peak depositing icy spray into the cockpit. There are shipwrecks marked on the chart all around us, it's a dangerous coastline. A few hours later we get to the entrance to the Delaware river and turn north once again motoring directly into the breeze. The river is wide with the low banks scarcely visible on each horizon. It's reminiscent of sailing in the North Sea – an endless expanse of shallow brown water punctuated by a series of navigation buoys. Bizarre shapes appear on the horizon in the otherwise empty seascape. These gradually resolve into strange-shaped beacons marking the shallows either side of the dredged channel. In the afternoon the tide turns, and we struggle to make four knots, pushing against wind and current.

We inch up the channel noting each marker as we pass it. Red markers on our starboard side – confusingly the opposite way around from Australia and Europe – and green to port; both streaked white with seagull shit. Every so often a ship passes us, heading up the river towards Philadelphia and we push to the edge of the deep water to allow it plenty of room. Evening falls and the physical shapes of the buoys fade into the twilight, replaced with a series of flashing red and green lights.

Around 11.00pm we're near the top of the river opposite the bright lights of the Salem nuclear power station. There's plenty of traffic on the water keeping us on our toes; tugs pushing barges showing three white lights on their mastheads, gigantic container vessels and smaller coasters loom out of the darkness. We debate about anchoring for the night –

but there's nowhere sheltered, and the breeze is whipping up an uncomfortable chop. It's better to push on through the Chesapeake and Delaware canal and anchor somewhere quieter in Chesapeake Bay.

The canal carries heavy shipping and is narrow in places, so we're supposed to call and get clearance to go through from the canal authorities. No one responds to our VHF call at that time of the night, so we watch the traffic on the AIS and do slow circles for an hour until the route is clear. Once in the canal, we have the current in our favour, so we glide silently along a smooth corridor of water marked on each side by amber lights. I glance upwards as we pass underneath each of the five bridges spread out over the fourteen-mile passage. We have checked and double checked the clearance on the chart, but the top of the mast still seems awfully close to the steel frame of each span.

The canal was dug 200 years ago, 'when labour was cheap' remarks Kent. The US Corps of Engineers has improved it since, and it is deep right up to the banks. This is a good thing as three quarters of the way along we meet a huge car carrier coming the other way. 190 metres long with a pilot boat attached to one side, the vessel takes up most of the width of the canal. The pilot calls us on the radio and instructs us to pass on his starboard side, so we squeeze up as close to the bank as possible as the behemoth moves past us in the darkness. Soon after, the canal opens out into a wider channel leading into the top of Chesapeake Bay. We push on a little further and anchor in the sheltered Sassafras River at around 3.00am.

We wake up late to a bright cold day. We're moored in a bight on the river – in the centre of the channel, but there's no traffic. The banks are heavily wooded – most of the trees have now lost their leaves, but a few still showing the last of their autumn colours. There are a few houses running onto the grey-green water, possible holiday dwellings as we can't see any sign of life. After breakfast we bring up the anchor, covered in thick mud that's difficult to wash off and we're scrubbing the deck as we head out into the Chesapeake once again. With the wind behind us the day soon warms up as we head along the bay and under the impressively named William Preston Lane Jr. Memorial Bay Bridge. This tongue twister of a bridge spans four miles across Chesapeake Bay and was the longest cross water bridge in the world when it was built in 1952. Once past it we turn to the west and drop anchor off the US Naval Academy at Annapolis.

Nicole is now a full-fledged Hurricane so we're in no hurry to head south, instead we use the time to make some repairs. We fix the mizzen boom gooseneck, it's connected to the mast via a ball and socket joint, and we hammer the stainless-steel back into place. That sorted, we turn our attention to the leaking steering system. It appears the seals on the hydraulic ram have gone, perhaps because I've pumped too much grease into it when lubricating the system. Kent disappears into the lazarette, the content of the locker piled high on the aft deck. There's the occasional request for a wrench or a hammer, but mostly all we hear for the next couple of hours are muffled curses. Eventually he emerges triumphant with the ram in his hands and takes it ashore to be repaired.

We also take the opportunity to catch up with an old friend who lives outside Washington DC. We haven't seen Will for 25 years, so it's wonderful to catch up over a long lunch and reminisce about family and friends. He's had an extraordinary life since we last saw him; at one stage he commanded the Scots Guards before leaving the army to work for a quasi-mercenary organisation in the US, providing security services in Iraq and Afghanistan. We're both godparents to each other's children but we've been hopeless on that score having lost touch with each other after he divorced. He seems unchanged by the past quarter century and it's a little surreal seeing him in this new context. Sadly, we don't get to meet his new wife, but we finish lunch with lots of entreaties to come and visit us in the Caribbean.

Our stay in Annapolis extends longer than planned. The hydraulic steering ram takes a few days to be repaired and when Kent refits it another leak materialises – this time from a different spot – so perhaps I'm off the hook for over-greasing. We take it back to the machinery shop for more work only to discover yet another leak on one of the fittings. Eventually, after a third attempt the equipment seems to be fixed. We celebrate Kent's 60th birthday with a long lunch in town. We have been trying to get him some Dubarry seaboots for his birthday but have been unable to find any. At the birthday lunch we're joined by Ken, the skipper of an American yacht moored on the town quay and his daughter Asia who we'd met at the harbourmaster's office the previous day. Ken reveals he has a pair of brand-new Dubarrys that don't fit, and he goes off to grab them. Sure enough, they fit Kent perfectly and he hands them over. We end up in the saloon of their yacht for a few drinks at the end of the lunch – by which time it's well into the evening.

It's a long week and we get a bit of cabin fever at times. There's a couple of tense moments between Kent and Colleen which is awkward for the rest of us given our close quarters. There are eight of us on board and although everyone is trying hard to get along, the confined space and lack of privacy aboard can act as a pressure cooker. We take some time out to visit the US Naval Academy, adjacent to where we're moored. You show a passport and go through airport style security to get in, but once inside visitors are free to wander almost anywhere. It seems very lax compared with the security at Sandhurst, where

I attended as an officer cadet thirty years ago. The grounds are immaculate with wide paths and manicured green lawns. Every so often classes change over, and we watch uniformed midshipmen hustle past at the double. There is an interesting museum of US Naval history, and we learn about John Paul Jones, a Revolutionary War hero who became known as the father of the US Navy. Til's interested to note he originally came from Arbigland in Scotland – a tiny place that's also the family home of a former boyfriend.

After a week at anchor, we're ready to move on. There's a stiff breeze from the north and it's cold. The weather app on my phone says 5 degrees Celsius, but feels like minus 2, so the sooner we head south the better. The route to the Caribbean is a well-trodden path as many yachts migrate south to avoid the frigid US winter. It's not an easy trip however, as you don't want to get to the Caribbean before December to avoid the hurricane season. This means leaving the US in late autumn or early winter by which time it's cold and there can be fierce gales in the north Atlantic. The gulf stream complicates things further. If this northerly flowing current meets strong winds going the other way, it becomes dangerously rough. Traditionally, the route from New England is via Bermuda, but the thinking is changing with more people now heading along the coast as far as South Carolina before striking out southeast and making directly for the islands.

We're keen to see Bermuda if we can and calling in there would break up a long ocean crossing. We pour over the synoptic charts like witch doctors trying to make sense of obscure runes. The weather is a little unsettled, but the forecast seems ok for the next few days, so we'll leave mainland US from Chesapeake Bay and head offshore towards Bermuda. It's about 700 miles to Bermuda so should take us around four or five days. If things go to plan, we'll call in there. If not, we have plenty of food on board and can always bypass it and head direct to the Caribbean.

We leave Annapolis at lunchtime under mizzen and genoa and make good progress south anchoring for the night near the mouth of the Patuxent River. We don't hang around there, continuing at sunrise the next morning in cold breezy conditions. All day we follow the line of green and red buoys marking the shipping channel which meanders from one side of the wide bay to the other and it's not until dusk we finally reach the southern end of Chesapeake Bay. The channel is busy with plenty of traffic heading into the bustling port of Norfolk. There's a big naval base and a huge aircraft carrier is silhouetted against the night sky. We take the north side of the channel, ducking into a promising looking inlet. It runs alongside Fort Munroe, a historic American Civil War site. This part of the US is redolent with history, many of the names and places evocative of the struggles between early colonists and the indigenous inhabitants or the later civil war battles between peoples with such obdurately opposing views. It would be nice to come back when it's warmer and explore more. It's difficult to pick out the channel markers against the city lights, so we inch our way in, eyes straining in the darkness eventually dropping anchor in a sheltered pool next to a busy highway. It's our last night in the US and so we go ashore for dinner, finding a low key, traditional southern diner. Shrimps and grits are the main item on the menu.

Next morning, we wake to see a well-equipped yacht sitting at a strange angle, hard against the seawall. We hadn't seen it coming in so it must have run aground during the night. The coastguard arrives and we later hear the yacht had transmission problems while trying to anchor – although there's no explanation how they managed to run on the rocks. It's a good reminder not to take anchoring too cheaply. There are the usual last-minute jobs to attend to and it's not until mid-afternoon we winch the dinghy back on board and raise the anchor. It's a beautiful sunny day but cold with a biting wind. We read online several feet of snow have fallen in New York; strange to think we sailed through there less than a fortnight ago.

Sailing from Annapolis we've had the bay largely to ourselves. At the southern end, things are very different and it's a busy highway. There are no other yachts out on the water, but plenty of other traffic; fishing boats, tugs pulling barges and vast container ships which appear from nowhere, rapidly overhauling us. Most vessels have AIS, an automatic vessel tracking system, so they show up on our chart plotter as black triangles moving across the screen. The system gives other useful information, indicating how close the vessel will get to us if we both stay on our current bearing and when that will be. It's all helpful, but nothing beats keeping a good lookout. At the entrance, 12 miles wide, there's a bridge which runs all the way across the bay. Every so often the bridge terminates in man-made islands and the road disappears below the surface and into a tunnel creating gaps for shipping and we slip quietly through one of these and out into the open ocean.

Dusk sees us off Cape Henry, a watery sun sinking below the horizon and the lights of mainland USA gradually fade behind us. I'm on watch with RL once again – the shifts are 3 hours on and 6 hours off, so there's plenty of opportunity to sleep although it takes a while to get into the rhythm. The first few hours we move past a series of moored ships waiting for space at their designated port inside the bay. They are huge – in some cases almost 400M long and lit up like Christmas trees so easy to keep clear of. We run the radar as well as the AIS on the plotter to make sure we don't accidentally bump into an unlit trawler but as we get further offshore the seas are empty. Our first night watch is bitterly cold but by the morning the temperature has risen and for the first time in a couple of weeks it's pleasant in the sun as we enter the Gulf Stream. There's no change in the wave formation, no visible sign we're in the current, just a very welcome warmth.

The second night passes without incident but shortly after dawn a front comes through. We watch it approaching on the radar, a line of fuzzy blue and orange pixels and we shorten sail before the wind and rain hits. The rain passes quickly but the wind persists through the day pushing the sea into an ugly lumpy mess; the 40-ton boat twists and rolls uncomfortably.

The increased seaway and strong winds have the autopilot working hard when mid-afternoon and without any warning, the steering fails again. The boat rounds to the wind and the sails flog in a thundering tumult as we dig through the lazarette to close off the hydraulic valve. Perched at the back of the boat, we revert to hand steering from the emergency tiller once more. The emergency tiller fits directly on the top of the rudder stock, there are no gears or leverage to lessen the force of the water and it's hard work keeping the boat straight in these big seas. It takes concentration and a lot of physical effort. We manage alright during the daylight, but it becomes much harder once darkness falls. The helmsman can't see the boat's track on the plotter and it's also hard to see the wind indicator from his position at the stern. The night is pitch black with no stars to line up against and it's extremely difficult to maintain a straight course. To make life harder we have the genoa poled out and are heading downwind in big seas with the boat surging close to the gybe mark. There's the hiss of breaking waves behind the helmsman and foaming white crests appear out of the darkness, roil alongside the boat before disappearing back into the blackness. We have a preventer on the boom but we're unable to avoid several accidental gybes causing the sails to slam across and we break some of the expensive batten cars.

We do half hour shifts on the tiller which is about the limit of our concentration.

Whilst all this is going on, Kent is below trying to work on the broken steering. It seems one of the copper hydraulic pipes is cracked and leaking. It's unclear whether this has been the problem all along or whether this is a new issue exacerbated by fixing the previous issues. It is in an extremely difficult place to get to – between the back cabin and the lazarette. Kent cuts the broken section of pipe and uses some rubber hose with multiple hose clamps to sheath the damaged part. All this takes a long time – but eventually he succeeds in temporarily fixing the leak and stabilising the system so it can withstand the pressure generated by the steering ram. We bleed the system and refill it with the last of the remaining hydraulic oil. Amazingly it holds and with relief we revert to the wheel once again. It holds through the remaining darkness and all the next day and night. We check the oil level periodically and it gradually becomes lower. We have no more fluid to refill it so keep the emergency tiller ready to go.

On the morning of the fourth day, it's cloudy with some drizzle. The visibility comes and goes but on the eastern horizon there are several faint grey smudges which look to be more than cloud. It takes a while before we're certain, but gradually these resolve into distinct rocky patches. 'Land ho!' In the drizzle it's not the sparkling aquamarine paradise from the brochure, but it's Bermuda nevertheless, and by mid-afternoon we're making our way through the narrow man-made channel into the lagoon at St Georges.

Brightly painted houses with white roofs look out onto a small port with anchored yachts and working boats in milky-blue water. We have been directed by Bermuda Radio to make our way to the customs office, so we hoist the yellow quarantine flag and moor up alongside Customs House. On the wharf is a formidable looking lady wearing a uniform with enough stripes and gold braid to rival an Admiral. She barks instructions at us and we dutifully hand over our passports. After filling in a few forms we're in.

The harbour master directs us to a berth on the town quay. We're allocated an extremely tight spot behind the pilot boat and in front of an American yacht with less than six inches to spare. It takes a bit of toing and fro-ing and provides good entertainment for the small crowd that forms on the wharf. They nearly get more than they bargain for when our steering fails once again but we're well practiced at the drill now and seamlessly move to the tiller and soon after we're secure against the dock.

The following morning, Til and I take the bus to the capital, Hamilton. It's a sociable trip as our fellow passengers are chatty as the small bus winds along the length of the island through the persistent rain. Whenever a new passenger gets on everyone greets them with a cheery good morning and there's plenty of good-humoured laughing and joking. We splash along the road, making our way around a series of coves and past well-built houses surrounded by lush green vegetation before arriving in a bustling, modern city. We've been tasked with getting some replacement hydraulic hoses for the troubled steering system from an industrial shop we've identified online. What we thought would be a straightforward assignment becomes complicated as the shop has no stock and we're directed to several different industrial supply outlets in the seedier suburbs of Hamilton. Although the prices are sky-high, and parts of the city are very cosmopolitan, we are on an island and supplies are limited. The people we talk to are friendly and keen to help – but it's hard to explain exactly what we want. In the end, we cobble together an approximation of what Kent has requested as well as buying a 5-gallon bucket of hydraulic oil. We become friendly with the team in the original shop, and they give us a lift back to the bus stop in the rain. I get a dirty look from the bus driver when I board with my large bucket of oil – but a smiling local lady pats the seat next to me and I cradle it on my knees. I have her life history by the time we're back in St Georges.

We've been checking the weather closely for the next leg south and it's looking unsettled. It seems there could be a weather window over the next day or so, but afterwards it deteriorates again. If we don't go shortly, we will likely be stuck in Bermuda for a couple of weeks. Bermuda is close to being the most expensive place on the planet and we're not keen to hang around longer than we must.

There's a bit to do before we can go, we need to fit the new hydraulic hoses for the steering system as well as repair a host of other smaller breakages. We also reprovision for the 800-mile crossing to the Caribbean. All this takes time and it's not until late the following evening we're ready to leave. Kent takes our passports around to customs house to clear us out and we motor across to the fuel wharf for a final top up of diesel. We're the last customers of the day for the fuel berth and the staff stand around impatiently waiting to go home while our tanks fill. A brisk onshore breeze pins us onto the wharf, and it takes some nifty fender work to avoid crunching the paintwork as we motor backwards into the lagoon.

We head back through the cut in darkness and for a while we're hard on the wind as we clear the shoal waters fringing the island. It's horribly choppy and the boat pitches and rolls as we bash through the waves. It's Thanksgiving Day and somehow, Til produces an amazing dinner in these conditions juggling pots trying to throw themselves off the stovetop. We eat it in the cockpit, the lights of Bermuda fading into the distance.

The sea smooths out as we bear away to the south, the wind

is on the beam and the sky is clear with a million stars. It should be a perfect night's sailing but the inspection hatch on one of the port fuel tanks is leaking and we have diesel sloshing about in the bilge. We were aware of this problem and tried to isolate this tank when we refuelled, but the valve must have failed as the tank filled anyway. There's a lot of swearing as Kent pumps this out and painstakingly re-taps the screws to better secure the hatch.

On Friday we download the latest weather update, and the forecast has changed. There is now a series of unpleasant looking low-pressure systems sweeping over Bermuda with strong winds forecast. Because of our late departure we are a little closer to the system than we'd like to be. We push south as fast as possible, but the wind is now against us, and we have 24 hours of motor sailing into rough seas. The boat is incredibly wet – the deck under tonnes of green water as the bow plunges into each wave and water sweeps back across the vessel. The low dodger provides little shelter for the helmsman in the cockpit. A series of intense squalls with heavy rain sweep across, adding to the misery.

The cabin below quickly turns into a wet mess as water finds its way in through air-vents, hatches and through fittings. The motion is so bad the forward berths are untenable, and bodies spread out across the saloon trying to find a dryish place to rest. This continues all night; there's not much sleep as the boat crashes to windward slamming off each wave with a juddering bang.

Eventually we get clear of the system and the wind shifts through 180 degrees and comes behind us before dying to a light breeze. It's a big improvement as there's no longer water coming into the boat but we roll uncomfortably with the sails slamming. We furl the headsail to try and minimise the wear and tear on the gear.

At some stage during the third night the wind fills from the northeast, and we talk hopefully about this being the start of the trades. We shake the reef out of the main we've carried since Newport. The day is sparkling – blue skies and a steady breeze and the boat quickly transforms into a laundry with mattresses and bedding airing on the deck and on makeshift washing lines. Thomas loses his sleeping bag overboard in the building breeze. We have too many preventers attached to be able to turn around and pick it up, so it's gone forever along with the bucket I lost the previous day. The other excitement is we finally catch not one fish – but two! There's an excited shout of 'Fish on!' as first a beautiful yellow and green mahi mahi slams into one of our lures. Half an hour later we pull out a silver wahoo on the other one. Fish on the menu tonight.

For this leg, I'm sharing a watch with Jeff; he's an entertaining companion, and the night hours fly by. He tells me how, after an impoverished start, his father made a lot of money identifying an enzyme now widely used in potato farming, protecting against blight. The family bought a lodge in the wilderness in Alaska about 50 miles from Denali which Jeff ended up running for several years. The winter there is long and harsh, temperatures regularly dropping to minus 50 or lower. The lodge could only be resupplied by air and the relief plane couldn't operate at those extreme temperatures, so they were often cut off for long periods. Jeff separated from his wife, so he was there alone with his young daughter for much of the time. At one point there was an awful disaster with the supply plane crashing on take-off in freezing conditions, killing the pilot. I tell him he should write a book. It would be a good read.

The rest of the trip is uneventful. The promising trade wind fades, and we motor across a glassy sea for the best part of 48 hours. The surface of the water a satin sheet undulating gently in the ocean swell. We troll with two lines but there are no more fish. Perhaps they are put off by the sound of the engine. We know it should be about the journey more than the destination, but we can't help counting off the miles and marking the lines of latitude as they pass. We also try our hands at noon day sun sights with the sextant. RL flukes it – coming in 4 miles from our actual latitude – the rest of us end up with an error of around a degree. Luckily, we're not reliant on this to find our way to the islands! Eventually as evening is falling on the fifth day, we sight Sombrero Island and a little later the faint outline of Anguilla. A long low island that appears briefly before fading into the gloaming. A light breeze has sprung up and we turn the engines off and glide the last few miles gently in the moonlight. Relying on the GPS we pass between two unlit islands and around the western end of Anguilla looking for a white flashing light that no longer exists. Finally, a short fetch up the channel and we nose our way into the anchorage at Grand Case in the French side of St Martin at around 10.00pm.

DECEMBER

Grand Case is a laid-back little town. There is one waterfront street with bars and restaurants and a few touristy boutiques. Most are a bit run down and there are some derelict buildings – courtesy of a hurricane that came through a few years ago. Walking inland away from the waterfront it's a rabbit warren of narrow streets and decrepit houses. It has a third world feel with low hanging power lines and ill sited billboards, but the atmosphere is friendly and unthreatening. There are some bars open to the street packed with locals. They have an easy manner and are quick to smile. The World Cup is streaming on TV, and everyone is engrossed. We have lunch on shore and enjoy a few rum punches. Evening seems to come quickly, and we retreat to the yacht while we still can.

Next day we motor a few miles to Marigot Bay. It's crowded

with tourists and lacks the charm of Grand Case and is not as friendly. We browse the markets and find the well-stocked chandlery. They also sell beer, as all good chandleries should, so we enjoy a cold refreshment while browsing the aisles full of ropes and shackles. After lunch in a touristy eatery – goat curry with rice is surprisingly delicious – we walk up the hill to the fort above the town. The French tricolour is flying from the flagpole on top of the fort – Cochrane would have had something to say about that.

Back at the boat that evening we pull up the anchor and head off in the dusk for Antigua, ninety miles away. We run down the lee of the island eating dinner in the sheltered water before we revert to three-hour watches once again. Once we get to the southern tip, we lose the protection of the land and we're back on the wind. It's a warm night however and the navigation is easy as we can see the lights of various islands. We pass St Barts, and later Nevis in the distance off to starboard as we head towards the loom of Antigua over the horizon. There's a bit of traffic to avoid as we plough through the darkness; cruise ships moving to their next destination, fishing boats and a naval warship all make sure we don't doze off. At dawn we're 15 miles from our destination and we gradually close with the arid hills of southern Antigua.

It's difficult to make out English Harbour until we're almost there. The narrow entrance to this beautiful inlet is hidden between rugged craggy slopes. The channel zigzags in and the swell quickly smooths out into a sheltered waterway lined with expensive looking superyachts. It's hard to imagine how Nelson bought his fleet of square riggers into such a tight space. We anchor near the entrance at Freemans Bay and dinghy in to go through the check-in process. This involves shuttling between 4 different offices – health, port authority, customs and immigration. It takes a while and there's a lot of stamping of paperwork and passports but eventually we're done.

In the evening we bring El Oro around to neighbouring Falmouth harbour. We switch into holiday mode with drinks in the Antigua yacht club followed by a barbeque dinner with margaritas and pina coladas. It starts to rain and RL calls Kent, who has stayed on the boat, on the handheld VHF to ask if he could move his underwear left drying on the rail. He makes the call on channel 16, the public calling channel, earning a sharp rebuke in response. Eventually we stagger back to the yacht leaving RL and Thomas to gate crash a superyacht party.

We're all slow the next day. Kent changes the oil in all three engines and replaces all the filters. I try and watch what he's doing in the tight engine room space as next time will be my turn. We check out and are stung with US$180 departure tax after paying an entry fee of US$200 the day before. Antigua is by far the most expensive island to get in and out of. We motor slowly out of Falmouth and make our way against the wind for an hour to Nonsuch Bay on the east coast. Using the GPS, we wind our way in through a series of reefs on both sides. There's a wreck washed up on a rocky outcrop, a good reminder to concentrate on staying in the middle of the channel. We're on the windward side of the island and drop the anchor in a position that looks horribly exposed, it seems open to the ocean, but is sheltered behind the protective reef hidden under the surface. Going ashore at dusk we swim on an idyllic beach we have to ourselves.

The perfect evening turns sour when we get back to the boat. Colleen and Kent have a huge row and she ends up in floods of tears taking shelter in our cabin. Kent, tired and emotional, retreats to his cabin slamming the door behind him. The rest of us sit in the cockpit uncertain how to deal with the situation – the boat is too small for this sort of behaviour.

At dawn I'm waiting for him in the cockpit, and we have a

very direct conversation. He's gracious and apologetic, offering to leave the boat as soon as practicable and we agree Colleen should fly out in Guadeloupe if possible. It's good to clear the air, but also awkward as Kent is someone I respect. He has so much experience and he's someone I need to be able to call on in the next few months to discuss any issues with the boat, so I'm keen to maintain the relationship.

We leave early in the morning for Guadeloupe intending to stop at Deshaies, a deep indent on the northern end of the island. We get there around 2.00pm but quickly push on. Although we should be in the northeast trades, strangely the wind is blowing from the west leaving the anchorage exposed to the incoming swell. We make for Les Saintes, a group of islands a few miles to the south of Guadeloupe. Like so many of these islands they've been contested by the big European powers who were desperate to hold onto the wealth generated by sugar and spices, built on the back of slavery. This little group is the site of the largest naval battle in Caribbean history – between the British under Admiral Rodney and the French fleet under Compte de Grass. We get there in the dark, nosing our way in slowly, trying to pick out the navigation lights against the bright lights from onshore bars and restaurants. We inch pass an unlit isolated danger mark sitting on top of a shoal and drop anchor in a busy harbour surrounded by moored vessels.

In the morning we go ashore to complete the check-in formalities. In the French islands the customs process is managed by third parties and in Les Saintes, it's done in a café above a row of shops. The sign on the door says they're closed until 2.00pm so Til and I take the time to walk up to one of the forts overlooking the bay. It's a hard slog in the heat; the original builders must have had a tough job dragging the stone slabs to the top of the hill. The views are spectacular – we can see Guadeloupe to the north, Dominica to the south and various smaller islands to the east, all surrounded by sparkling blue water.

That night the wind drops, and we roll heavily as El Oro lies sideways on to the westerly swell. It doesn't take much discussion to move on and we pull the anchor up at 2.00am to head for our next destination, Dominica. Motoring through the rest of the night we arrive at Prince Rupert Bay on the north-eastern end of the island soon after first light. The weather pattern is still contrary with no sign of the trades, so the anchorage is rolly, but not as bad as Les Saintes.

We haven't been anchored long before we're visited by a boat boy in a brightly coloured local boat who introduces himself as Elvis. We decline his services for now and head ashore for the check-in which is in the run-down customs shed near the commercial wharf. It's impossible to leave the dinghy at the wharf due to the swell so I make a jump for it, timing the surge of the wave to step out onto the jetty leaving Kent to wait offshore. The customs process is efficient, if old fashioned. There are no computers here – everything filled out longhand with carbon copies. On Kent's advice, I've denoted most of our party as passengers, but the large and slightly intimidating official frowns as he stabs at my form with a pencil, telling me passengers must go through immigration and pay arrival and departure tax.

'Erm, how about I designate them as crew?' I ask. Wordlessly he hands me back the form and I cross out passenger and replace with crew. There's nothing to pay.

There's no major international airport on Dominica so the island is less commercialised than its neighbours. It's poorer than some of the other islands and many buildings show signs of disrepair, but there's a strong sense of civic pride. Gardens are tended and the streets are largely free from litter. Billboards exhort people not to use plastic bags. We hire two cars – no deposit taken, no credit card shown and head off to do some exploring. The roads are narrow and edged with disconcertingly deep storm drains. The island itself is largely covered with thick jungle and rises to over 4,000 ft on the central peaks. We wind our way around these and over to the west coast before tracking back inland. We find a crystal-clear mountain stream cascading through pipes under the road into a deep pool and stop for a swim. Lunch is at a wayside stop: Patrick's Restaurant and Bar. Restaurant is perhaps an overstatement – the place is really a grimy shack with an eclectic miscellany of furniture and some stray cats. We're the only diners and Patrick seems a bit surprised by our presence, but he rustles up some delicious fried chicken and fish. Afterwards we head onto the Emerald pools, a series of tumbling green waterfalls cutting through the jungle and a good spot for another plunge. We're high in the mountains now and it's a lot cooler, but the water is still refreshing.

The road becomes rougher and rougher until it is little more than a deeply rutted track. At one stage we come to a construction zone where earthmoving vehicles have dug up the road even further. The surface is like a ploughed field, and it seems impossible we can get through, but we're in a rental car so we give it a go. Our lightweight Suzuki Ignis bounces across the ruts, and on we go. We have no map, and no mobile data so are navigating largely by the direction of the sun but there are few roads so we can't go far wrong. The low fuel light adds an element of stress for a time, but we freewheel to the coast and ask directions to a petrol station. There's some farce as none of us can open the fuel cap of the hire car – a crowd of locals assemble to try and assist and there's much laughter and joking as we eventually work it out.

Back on the boat we depart at dusk to continue south; this time our destination is Le Marin at the southern end of Martinique. It's another perfect moonlit night for a sail – but unfortunately there's no wind so once again it's engines on.

Arriving at Le Marin is a huge contrast after low key Dominica. We motor into a sheltered anchorage through a winding channel towards a forest of masts. A line of palm trees which look like they've been transplanted from somewhere else, sit out the front of a Club Med resort. As we get closer inshore, there are yachts everywhere. Hundreds of them on swing moorings in different states of repair. We pass a few that have sunk; the top half of the mast protruding at a strange angle above the water. There are two huge marinas with row upon row of plastic cruising yachts and catamarans. Le Marin is a major yachting hub and a jump-off point for boats wanting to cruise the Windward Islands. It has a bustling charter industry. We avoid the crowds and find a secluded bay off to one side and drop the hook behind a band of coral, 50 metres from the shore.

Randel and Kent work on the boat – patching up the large and obvious holes in the topcoat with fresh blue paint. The paintwork has not survived three New England winters and is cracked and crazed with patches flaking off. Repainting will be a huge job but a temporary touch up will help. Whilst they're doing that, we head into town to check-in and do some shopping. The check in is managed through the marina office, it's quick and they only charge a €5 fee. It's quite the contrast with Antigua. From there we search out the boulangerie to stock up on baguettes and croissants. Martinique is an overseas department of France, and there's no mistaking it. The street signs are in the same font and layout as signs in mainland France and the brusque attitude of some of the shopkeepers is much the same.

Next day Thomas & Jeff depart and we're down to six. The boat is suddenly roomy, and it takes a little time to adjust to the new dynamic after living so tightly for so many weeks. After lunch we go to pull the anchor up but there's only a click from the solenoid and no movement in the winch. When we attach a handle and try to turn the windlass by hand we get some slight assistance from the motor, but it's not at all happy. We agree the best thing is to get to Rodney Bay, we can have a proper look at the problem there.

There's very little wind, and what's there is still unusually coming from the west, so we motor across the strait to St Lucia. The light fades and we eat underway enjoying a beautiful evening on the water. The lights along the shoreline get brighter as we approach, guiding us in and we nose our way into Rodney Bay in the darkness, picking our way through the anchored boats on radar. When we find a clear spot, we drop the anchor unsure whether the windlass motor will work in the morning. The beautiful evening turns into an uncomfortable, rolly night however as the swell curls around Fort Rodney and catches us side on; there's not a lot of sleep to be had.

In the morning it's bad news regarding the windlass. We try to bring up the anchor but even with manual assistance there's very little life in the motor. We press the 'up switch' but use a winch handle to turn the windlass. The motor provides the smallest amount of additional turning moment. It's hard work and slow. We call the marina to see if we can get a berth, but it's full; the ARC rally is in full swing with dozens of boats arriving from Europe so we can't go in there; the best thing is to try and get a mooring at Marigot Bay an hour to the south.

I've been to Marigot Bay before, in the early 1980s with my parents when we had to take shelter there from a tropical storm whilst chartering a yacht out of season. It's one of the very few hurricane holes on the west coast of St Lucia and a very sheltered spot. I was 16 and I can remember tying our yacht to the mangroves and lying on my bunk in oppressively hot and humid conditions with all the hatches tightly battened whilst torrential rain lashed down outside. Coming into Marigot Bay nearly 40 years later I can clearly recognise the bay and even the bar where we had rum punches in coconut shells all those years before. There has been a bit of development, but the place doesn't seem to have changed so much in the intervening years.

We moor fore and aft given the limited room to swing and Kent disappears into the forepeak to try and take the anchor winch apart. He spends much of the day struggling with it and eventually after a lot of swearing appears with the motor in hand. The motor is filled with grease that must have leaked from the gearbox. The motor is the problem, but the gearbox may also need repairing given it's been operating without any grease.

While we're moored in Marigot Bay, we're visited for the day by Randel's young kids. They clamber all over the boat disappearing down hatches and into lockers exploring every nook and cranny. Rahim spots the binoculars which he slings around his neck. He's also fascinated by a large magnifying glass in the navigation table and peers through it like a young Sherlock Holmes. To keep them entertained, Til gets out her coloured pencils and Alicia draws a picture of her brother. RL comes over to admire it and then asks her if she'll do a portrait of him. She looks him up and down very seriously and then glances at the palette. 'Sorry, no I can't,' she replies. 'I don't have any white.'

That evening we go ashore for happy hour where the bar is serving two for one drinks. Afterwards we come back to the boat for unhappy hour. Kent and Colleen have another huge row and she retreats to her cabin slamming the door with a bang. RL goes up on deck with his speaker and plays music outside our cabin late into the night. Exasperated, Til gives him an earful and eventually everyone retreats to bed.

In the morning there are a few sheepish people worried about how much of the previous night's angst has been carried over. There are some muttered apologies and things smooth over quickly, helped by the fact that Kent takes Colleen to Castries by dinghy where she catches a ferry to Martinique and from there a flight back to France. Afterwards we stay another, quieter night in Marigot Bay before heading further along the coast to Soufriere to drop off Randel's dinghy and the one surviving pumpkin that's made it across from Newport.

Soufriere Bay is stunning; the town nestling in a carpet of thick green jungle backed by the dramatic vertical cliffs of the Pitons. The water is deep right up to the shore and azure blue. The town itself is very local – there's no development for tourists and the narrow streets are bustling with cars and people. There are open drains with unpleasant grey slime at the bottom and the smells of warm jungle, cooking and sewage all combine into a heady cocktail. There are pigs nosing about in the mud at the water's edge and the place has an edgy energy. You could have great fun, or you might get mugged. After dropping off the dinghy with Randel and his brother TJ, we find a supermarket and do some shopping for a few basics before hopping back on the yacht.

We make our way back towards Rodney Bay – we're keen to test out the motor for the windlass now that Kent has cleaned it out and reassembled it. On the way the engines both overheat, and we shut them off. We crossed a band of sargasso weed leaving Soufriere Bay and this has blocked the water intake. The suction from the engine makes it hard to remove the plastic caps on the top of the filters, but we leverage them off with a screwdriver and scoop out the weed.

We anchor in the dark once again in Rodney Bay. The wind has come back around to the more usual north-easterly direction and the swell is much more comfortable. The winch works well dropping the chain – we'll need to wait until the morning to see if it is equally happy retrieving it. Optimistically we speculate the problem is solved and now the grease is removed from the motor it will be fine.

In the morning our misplaced optimism is quickly cut short. The winch runs normally for a few moments before there's acrid smell of burning electrics, a thin wisp of smoke coiling up from the hawser pipe. Soon afterwards it cuts out altogether and with dismay, we retrieve the heavy anchor and chain by hand using the snubber line taken back to the halyard winch on the mast. It's a longwinded process and hard work, but it gets the anchor up.

The marina is still officially full, but they take pity on us and give us a berth right out on the end of the unfashionable J arm. It's shallow; the depth reads 0.0M under the keel, but we seem to be afloat. There aren't many other private yachts here – mainly commercial party boats including the infamous Pearl – a pirate ship used in the Pirates of the Caribbean movies that now plays loud thumping music at all hours of the day and night. We don't care, we're simply grateful for a place to be able to tie up.

Next day Kent departs for Italy. We do a last-minute shopping trip to buy him some bags in the hope he'll take more stuff off the boat and a little later he's gone, leaving a whirlwind of chaos behind him. With all the anchor problems it's late in the day when he starts packing and the boat is turned upside down as he searches for his stuff. Randel takes him to the airport, and we're left by ourselves.

It's strange having waited for this moment for so long. We should be celebrating; we're finally in charge of El Oro but I can't get excited. Instead, I'm worried we'll be unable to resolve the anchor problems. Without a windlass we're effectively grounded. We've proven we can anchor manually but hauling up the 50kg hook and heavy chain is a huge effort and not feasible with an inexperienced crew. It's also not safe; if the anchor drags, or if the weather changes, we may need to bring it up quickly. We're in the run up to Christmas, businesses are closing, and there's not much in the way of spares or replacements available in St Lucia. It could take weeks to get fixed and we have Kate arriving the next day followed by Toby and Alexis the next and Sarah from Rhode Island the day after. It's not going to be much fun if we're stuck in the marina. It's also expensive at over US$100 a night and we could be here for a long time.

Next morning after tidying up we go and see Ulrich who runs the Yacht Services at Rodney Bay and who has done work for Tim in the past. He's a tall weary looking Austrian who settled in St Lucia twenty years ago but now seems worn down by the challenges of trying to run a business on this island. We discuss the situation, and he tells us there's no way the gearbox will be in working order after what it's been through. It will need to come out and be rebuilt. The motor will also likely need replacing.

This is a blow as Kent has told us it will be near to impossible to remove the gearbox and it may have been epoxied into the hull. However, we set to work on the task. It's hard to tell exactly how it's connected so we end up removing everything in the vicinity that might be holding it in including the inner forestay and a hefty metal plate on the underside of the deck. It all takes a long time and is hot sweaty work and by lunchtime we don't seem any closer to removing it. Eventually we take some advice from Laurence, a local engineer who works for Ulrich. He's doing some work on the boat next door, but he sticks his head into our anchor locker to survey the situation. Satisfied we've removed anything that might be securing the unit to the deck he takes a lump hammer and a block of wood and bangs the top of the driveshaft firmly. After a few blows it shifts a millimetre or two and suddenly it's loose and dropping into RL's lap in the anchor locker.

Laurence takes the gearbox to his workshop where he dismantles it. Later I sit in Ulrich's office, his desk covered in assorted paperwork and metal cogs. 'How technical are you?' he asks.

'Not very,' I reply. He shakes his head and types up a list of parts which he prints and hands to me.

There are a series of bearings, both open and closed, as well as some oil seals on the list. He explains he doesn't have them in stock but if I can source them, he will do his best to rebuild the gearbox.

'Do you think I'll find them on the island?' I ask. Ulrich shrugs and tells me I can try. He doesn't sound very hopeful but points me in the direction of some hardware stores.

Randel and I head off in his battered Suzuki Vitara to see what we can find. We call into the hardware store Ulrich has mentioned but they don't have anything remotely resembling what we need but suggest we look at car part outlets instead. It seems there are dozens of these stores all over St Lucia and we visit most of them over the next six hours. Most have the same format; a grimy shopfront advertising various lubricants, behind which is a counter barred off to the public and manned by a bored attendant who shakes his or her head nonchalantly when we proffer the list of parts needed. Occasionally we encounter someone a little more proactive who suggests somewhere else we might look.

After a couple of hours with no hint of success I'm a bit flat. It's hot, the traffic is heavy, and it doesn't seem as if any of these items exist on this island. We come out of yet another parts centre having been directed to somewhere obscure on the other side of town when we notice an outlet a hundred metres up the road that we missed on the way down. It's the usual format, perhaps a little grungier than average but the guy behind the counter is friendly and takes my piece of paper. He consults a well-thumbed directory and disappears into the back room. A few moments later he re-emerges: 'was it a 7004 you needed?' I shrug as the number doesn't correspond to what I have on my list – but he's not discouraged and ducks back into his storeroom. When he comes back, he has in his hand several of the bearings we need. He can't help with the seals, but he directs us to some other outlets we can try.

After this it's like the veil has been lifted. We have success in several stores and end up sourcing all the bearings we need and one out of the three seals. We never find the other two and by late afternoon we're exhausted and out of options so head back to Rodney Bay. I've no idea if Ulrich will be able to manage with what we've found.

Ulrich is full of smiles when I produce our haul of goodies; he seems surprised we've managed to get most of what's required, and he says he'll be able to work around the lack of seals. His team rebuild the gearbox and clean up the electric motor, but for some reason don't test it in the workshop.

When we come to re-install the gearbox, we find we have another problem. There seems no way to attach the gearbox and motor to the hull. Laurence calls round to see how we're getting on and he pokes his head into the anchor locker to have a look at the situation. We hear a muffled 'Oh bloody hell…' repeated over and over before he re-emerges. It seems during the removal process, when he was banging it with a hammer, part of the housing has sheared off due to the excessive corrosion. This housing is now stuck to the underside of a metal plate that mounts the windlass to the bottom of the deck. We eventually manage to lever the entire plate including the broken mount off the boat with a jemmy bar.

The problem is without the housing we can't attach the gearbox to the underside of the deck. To make matters worse we hook up the electric motor to the battery to check it's working and there's nothing. It's dead as a dodo. It looks like we need a new electric motor.

Whilst we're working on the windlass, RL's wife Kate flies in. We smile wryly as RL takes a cab to the airport to pick her up. He'd earlier befriended one of the local guys who hang around the marina selling the odd joint and bumming cash off rich yachties. His new friend offers to run him to the airport and RL comes back to the boat with a huge grin, skiting he's negotiated a fare of $50 for the round trip, about half the normal cost. The day before Kate arrives however, we're having a coffee with RL when we come across his new friend paralytically drunk. He can hardly walk, let alone drive. RL back peddles hard on the airport arrangement having to tell a few white lies to get out of having him drive.

The following day our friends from Hong Kong, Toby and Alexis, arrive via Miami. Sarah cancels as she has covid which is possibly a good thing given we're stuck for the moment. We are also due to be in Martinique in a couple of days to pick up our son Alfie who is on his way back to Australia to begin Uni having had a year working in the UK. Martinique is about 25 miles to the north; we need to get there and moor up safely without an anchor windlass.

Ulrich is a bit elusive, but we eventually pin him down. He says it might be possible to fix the electric motor, but he'll also keep an eye out for a replacement. He points us in the direction of Chinaman to try and weld up the aluminium housing so we can refix the unit back to the boat.

We've already met Chinaman when we first came into Rodney Bay a couple weeks earlier. He runs a machinery shop at the back of the boatyard that looks like something out of a Star Wars set. His workshop is a makeshift shed made from container walls and plastic tarpaulins and it is littered with metal pipes, sheets and offcuts. You must pick your way through these to get to the different machines which are in various states of repair. There are tools everywhere and at the back of the shed is a desk where Chinaman sits, presiding over his empire like some mafia boss. A large intimidating figure, it turns out he's not Chinese but from Guyana. He carries a Glock pistol openly in his jeans pocket. He will only accept cash, preferably in US dollars, something I discovered when we asked him to repair the lid of our leaking fuel tank when we arrived. I'm unsure whether Chinaman is a nickname I should use to his face, but fortunately he proffers a large, scarred hand and introduces himself to Til as Chinaman, so I gather it's OK.

We take the windlass to his workshop, and he summons his cousin Claudius to help us. Claudius has even more scars on his hands and arms than Chinaman; clearly occupational health and safety isn't a big concern here. He gets to work applying heat to the corroded housing to break it apart from the metal plate. From there he welds the two broken sections together. Chinaman comes over to check his homework and shoos him out of the chair. He mutters something about aluminium being very difficult to weld and sets to himself wielding the welding rods like a master craftsman. We could be back in business before too long.

Back at the marina we have more good news. Ulrich drops round proffering a new 24V electric motor he's found somewhere. It looks good, but the end of the motor that mates to the gearbox is different from the original and the driveshaft won't connect. It looks like a job for Chinaman.

We leave that team thinking about this and Toby and I go to check out so we can leave for Martinique. Unfortunately, we're behind the skipper of a huge superyacht with a big crew so the process takes forever. It's simpler than checking in, you only need to clear with customs and immigration but there are still four different forms to be completed and signed. There's a bit of a drama about Kate's passport as it seems she was never properly stamped into the country but eventually we get our clearance to leave.

Our next step is to refuel with duty free diesel. It's a big moment when we let go the lines and slowly ease out of the marina berth. It's the first time I've overseen El Oro underway and I'm nervous as although I've steered the boat for long periods on the voyage from the US, I have never practiced manoeuvring in and out of docks. El Oro's a long, heavy boat with no bow thruster, so this is not so easy, particularly in any sort of breeze.

We circle off the fuel wharf with several other boats ahead of us. There's one working bowser and it takes a while. Eventually, our turn comes around and we edge gently into the wharf allowing the breeze to gradually push us in. We pull up the floorboards, open all eight fuel tanks and take on 1,240L of fuel which takes a good hour, before shutting them all off again and heading out of the channel into Rodney Bay.

Crossing the bay, the water colour changes from turquoise to deep blue, and we hoist the mizzen and staysail before turning north around Fort Rodney and into the open sea towards Martinique. The boat dips to the swell and schools of flying fish leap out of the waves in front of us. The trade winds are blowing hard, and we surge forward at eight knots. Sea birds hover close to our masts, inches from the rigging, watching for the flying fish to burst out and glide forward over the waves. Picking a target, one will tuck in its wings and zero in on the fish hitting the water with a great splash before surfacing again, sometimes with fish in beak. Our guests go quiet and turn a little green in the rough seas.

It's about four hours across the channel to the port of Le Marin at the south-eastern corner of Martinique. Because clearing out and taking on fuel has taken longer than planned, we are on a tight deadline. We've booked a berth at the marina given we don't have a windlass, but the marina won't give us a pen number and we need to be there by 6.00pm at the latest. We did investigate taking a mooring, called a corps mort – or dead body in French, but we're told our boat is too big.

At quarter to six we're at the entrance to the channel and we call up the marina. They tell us to call again at the fuel wharf – but by the time we get there everyone's gone. There's another boat docked on the fuel wharf so we can't moor there, so we head off cautiously in the dusk to find an anchorage knowing we'll now have to raise and lower the anchor manually. The good thing is we've been here a few weeks before with Kent, so we know where to go. We have one shot, so we can't stuff it up. We manoeuvre slowly towards the reef and drop the hook in six metres of water.

Next day we book into the marina. To get the anchor up, we use the snubber line taken back to the halyard winch to take up around 5 meters at a time. We tie off the anchor and repeat the process. It takes a while, but we get there in the end. It's a bit like an old sailing ship with a capstan.

Getting into the marina berth is a little tricky – reversing into a narrow spot between two enormous yachts and picking up bow lines, European style. It's tense for a moment, as I struggle to keep the boat straight going astern, but we make it in gliding backwards without hitting our neighbours and tie up stern to the wharf.

The French islands intrigue us as they're such a blend of Europe and the Caribbean. They are distinctly different from their neighbours. Being overseas departments of France, and subsidised by the mother country, they seem on the surface to work more effectively than some of the other independent islands. The bureaucracy we see is less complex; it's quicker and easier to check in and out of the country. In Martinique, which we visit often, you can find most of the major French supermarkets which are well stocked. Browsing the aisles in air-conditioned comfort is like shopping anywhere in the western world; it's easy and food is plentiful. Down the road there's the boulangerie where the bread price is capped, and there's an array of French pastries. To our visitor's eyes however, the orderliness of Martinique seems to miss some of the colour and noise of the independent islands. What are the downsides from the lack of independence? Is it better to be independent and poor or absorbed into the colonising power and better off? With the language barrier it's difficult to ask the locals but I suspect if we did, they'd shrug and look perplexed. As far as we can see there isn't any desire to move to independence.

We take advantage of Toby being a French speaker and the good supermarkets to do our Christmas shopping, stocking up on wine and cheese as well as croissants and baguettes for breakfast. Chinaman has asked us to source some stainless-steel tubing for the pulpit which needs repairing after being damaged the previous season, so we also search for that – although we don't find it until the next morning and end up paying over the odds for the short length we require. In the evening Til and I take a cab to the airport and pick up Alfie who has flown in from London.

Next morning, we head back to St Lucia. It's blowing hard and the sea is lumpy, but the sail is exhilarating with the wind on our port quarter. We hit nine knots at times with mizzen and staysail set. Back at Rodney Bay we head into the marina again, getting more confident at docking. This time we've been upgraded and are allocated a spot on the superyacht arm. El Oro looks very small alongside the row of mega yachts, but she makes up for size with good looks. RL goes over to Chinaman's place and sure enough he has turned a new aluminium end to the electric motor, so it now fits to the gearbox. He brings the whole machine back to the boat and we spend a frustrating evening trying to fit it. We are contorted in the anchor locker wrestling with the windlass, but for some reason we can't get it to fit properly through the deck of the boat.

After a good night's sleep everything is much clearer. We can see the new weld has prevented the gearbox from seating properly against the underside of the deck. It's a simple job to take the unit out and grind off the excess weld material and refit it. There's a hiccup as we're not sure how to wire up the unit – but in a stroke of luck, a cheery electrician called Egbert swings by and connects us up in about five minutes. Hallelujah, the winch is now working and we're back in business.

It's Friday night which in Rodney Bay is the jump-up. Each Friday evening, the streets of Gros Islet, to the north of the marina, are shut off to vehicles and host a massive street party. Stalls selling spicy fried chicken and all manner of drinks line the centre of the road and gigantic speakers blare out loud Caribbean tunes. It's packed with revellers swaying to the music and everyone seems to be having a good time. There are drugs openly on offer and several times we're asked if we want ganja or Charlie. Randel warns us it can be dangerous for tourists, and we shouldn't be out after midnight. RL looks at him disdainfully, 'I'm definitely going to be out later than that' he retorts.

'Well, it might be OK, but make sure you stay out of the bushes' is the cryptic response.

Next morning, we're back at anchor in Rodney Bay and are about to head up the fort for a walk when Til announces the aft head is blocked. It's full to overflowing so I turn off the water and bail it out, while trying to flush the system. Unfortunately, it doesn't clear; I need to dismantle the pipework behind the loo to try and find the blockage. It turns out the plumbing is weird. The pipes go under the boat and all the way across to the other side where once upon a time there was a holding tank. From there, they dive back under the boat and join a hard pipe with several 90-degree bends before connecting to flexible pipe again and heading out to the seacock. Try as I might, I can't clear the blockage and I can't get to the pipe under our cabin. I'd need to remove the floor of the shower which looks to be permanently sealed to the boat. I try and rod it clear but end up covered in shit. It's hot, unpleasant work and extremely frustrating. In the end I seal off both ends of the offending pipe leaving the blockage there and bypass it altogether with a new length of pipe I find under RL's bunk. The new arrangement is much simpler, although I am worried we might get water flowing back into the boat when it heels over given the shorter scope – but we can cross that bridge later and I can always turn off the seacock.

After a big clean up and bailing out the very nasty bilge, filled with a mix of shit and hydraulic oil left over from the steering dramas, we are set to go. We hoist staysail and mizzen and head gently along the coast at under 4kts to Marigot Bay. It's very relaxing – and necessary to de-stress after our plumbing dramas. We anchor off Marigot Bay – it takes a couple of attempts as there's a steep underwater slope and the first time we drag as the anchor slips into deeper water. Til produces an amazing dinner of duck breast – courtesy of Auchan in Martinique.

In the morning we walk up the hill above the bay to Barry's shop to try and top up on a few supplies. The sign over the door announces it's Pam's community shop, but we learn from Eileen, who's managing the till, that Pam has recently died, and her son Barry has taken over the shop. Eileen is Barry's girlfriend and is proprietorial with the store. She's chatty and friendly although we don't come away with much as the shelves are mainly empty. Unfortunately, the bakery next door is also closed so it's not a very successful outing. We amble back down the hill, past several stalls selling assorted touristy gifts and back to the boat. The windlass works like a dream, and we bring the anchor up and sail to Soufriere arriving there at lunchtime.

We take a mooring off Sugar Beach between the two Pitons having been warned by Ulrich not to stay near the town for security reasons. In the past few months, several yachts have been robbed, some at gunpoint, by a gang operating off the beach. Sugar Beach is a stunning location, the sheer Pitons rising directly from the sea; deep blue water so clear you can see the bottom 20M below. The shoreline is rocky with beautiful sandy beaches. There's a well-maintained resort which isn't too precious about yachties using their beach and next to that, there's a good area for snorkelling along the base of the smaller Piton. The crystal-clear water is enticing and there are schools of brightly coloured fish but unfortunately most of the coral looks to be dead or dying. This seems to be the case wherever we go in the Caribbean. We read there are coral diseases originating in this region, decimating the reefs. The damage is exacerbated by global warming and pollution. It's a desperately sad situation.

The wind funnels through the gap in the Pitons in intense bullets pushing our 40-ton yacht to and fro like a child's toy. The mooring buoy is dragged underwater by the weight of the boat, but the cable holds firm. We speculate about what would happen if the mooring line broke and whether we would have time to react before the boat hit the shore.

It's Christmas eve and for dinner we feast on quail from Martinique, done in the oven and potatoes dauphinoise as well as an array of drinks. Toby has the galley set up like a bar and is offering a range of cocktails and wines which we partake of liberally.

We wake up to discover our fears about the mooring were justified. The catamaran on the mooring next to us has broken free in the night and ended up on the rocks. Some shellshocked Brazilians approach us in a dinghy having managed to get their boat off the rocks asking us if we have any epoxy to mend a hole in the hull that is now letting in water. We have a tube of waterweld on board which is supposed to work underwater so we give it to them, and they disappear back into their vessel which they have re-moored on another vacant buoy. An hour later we see them heading south towards the St Vincent channel – away from the charter base where they would have picked up their boat. Clearly keen not to let a few rocks ruin their holiday, they are soldiering on. Will the damage get picked up by the charter company or will it be a problem that haunts some future renters?

We have a Christmas morning swim and head back to the boat for lunch of giant Martinique prawns and homemade mayonnaise. We share presents – a Kris Kringle type affair with each donor having to produce an accompanying poem to reveal both recipient and donor. This is interpreted in lots of different ways but results in great hilarity and of course more drinks before afternoon siestas. I set an alarm on the GPS to alert us if we move from our mooring.

On Boxing Day, we say goodbye to Toby and Alexis – the latter now known as 'Alex Is' as this is how RL, who seems to have trouble with names, christens her. It's sad to see them go, they've been such enthusiastic crewmembers over the past week, and it seems despite some of the challenges they've enjoyed their stay. It has been lovely having them on board.

We cast off the mooring and motor around the corner to Malgretoute beach off Soufriere so we're in place to pick up

Randel the next day. This was the area Ulrich warned us to avoid. The ranger comes round to collect the mooring fee and we ask about the situation. 'Oh, it's OK now,' he says, writing out a receipt for our mooring. 'Those guys are now in prison – enjoying their ham and turkey on the inside.' This is accompanied with a huge belly laugh as if he's cracked the best joke in the world. Somewhat reassured, we hope he's right. There is lots of talk in the newspapers and in yachting forums about the skyrocketing crime rate in St Lucia. It's a problem the locals need to get sorted if they are going to keep attracting tourists, however the situation is likely a bit overblown. It seems most thefts are opportunist given the increasing poverty levels following covid and providing we take sensible precautions like lifting the dinghy out at night, leaving someone on board wherever possible and keeping valuables locked away, things should be OK. There are a huge number of yachts cruising here, a very small percentage report problems.

Aside from the boat boys who help us pick up our mooring we also have a steady stream of visitors throughout the day touting a range of merchandise from jewellery to ganja. Others come by offering to help find a taxi, organise a tour to the waterfall or visit the hot springs that bubble up from the volcano. Mostly we politely decline, although there's an old man in a yellow wooden dinghy selling fruit and vegetables who gives us a good price and we buy from him regularly. One day some kids come past on a paddleboard offering to take our rubbish ashore. After some brief haggling, we pass over 10EC, and a full garbage bag. There's lots of grinning and nodding when we ask them to make sure it goes into a bin. Later that afternoon we go for a walk along the beach and see our garbage bag in the bushes a few metres back from the water. We pick it up and take it to town where we put it in a skip.

In the morning we head into Soufriere in the dinghy and

meet Randel. I clear us out, not realising it's a public holiday which costs us an additional $100 fee, and we do a last-minute shop. Til tries to get some cash out of the ATM which promptly eats her card. The bank is closed for the holiday and we're leaving the country that morning so there's not much we can do apart from cancel the card.

We track parallel with the coast, motoring through the huge wind shadow cast by the Pitons and eventually into the St Vincent passage. Here the trade wind is blowing full strength and it's a boisterous reach across a lumpy sea. We're tired by the time we get into the lee of St Vincent and it's a relief to pull into Cumberland Bay to be met by an enthusiastic contingent of boat boys. We anchor close off the beach where a white-haired old man provides a line to tie our stern to a palm tree. The setting is magical. This side of St Vincent is rain soaked and the resulting vegetation is lush and green. The bay is a perfect horseshoe shape with a reef on both sides. A little before dusk we snorkel in the translucent water at the entrance to the bay and promise ourselves we'll be back for more in the morning.

We're enticed into a local bar behind our palm tree by a character in a pirate hat introducing himself as Captain Morgan. We seem to be the only guests in the pub although there are a few locals hanging around the fringe. We discover Captain Morgan's real name is Will and he joins us for a couple of beers. RL takes over the sounds for the pub. It's unclear what the locals think of his music taste, but Will enjoys it and produces some bongo drums and maracas for us to play along with.

Next morning it's raining steadily which seems to be standard weather for this locale, so we skip the snorkelling and head south, arriving at Bequia after lunch. This is the first of the Grenadines and is a focal point for visiting yachts. Off the township there is a huge bay crowded with yachts and we take some time to find a clear spot in the thicket of boats. We eventually drop our anchor in Princess Margaret Bay not far off the beach. It's easy to see why the place is so crowded; the island has an enticing, laid-back charm. We buy a couple of lobsters from a passing fisherman and cook them up for a delicious early dinner. Another local man stops by later to say he recognises our boat from the 1970s when it was owned by a Frenchman. Presumably Baron Bich's CFO.

Next day it's very windy but we're keen to look around the south of the island so we up anchor and motor past a long line of cliffs. There's the disconcerting sight of a smashed-up yacht crumpled at the foot of one of these cliffs, its mast at a crazy angle and we speculate about the circumstances that could have led to this; not something we want to emulate.

Turning the corner at the end of the cliff, we motor along the south coast past the airport. It's slow going against the howling gale funnelled between Bequia and the islands further south. We look at the anchorage off the old whaling station at Petit Nevis, but the surge is too strong and there are reefs on both sides so give up on that idea, instead heading into Friendship Bay. This is a deep scallop-shaped indent that is approached past a series of jagged rocky islets. The surf crashes clean over these; it's not a place for the steering or engines to fail. Once into the bay we gain shelter from the wind, but not from the swell that curves around the reef and rolls us sideways on. We endure this through an uncomfortable lunch lurching from side to side but are eventually driven out and end up returning to Princess Margaret Bay and find our way to the exact spot we left a few hours before.

In the morning we leave early for the 18-mile sail to Canouan. We can see the grey outline in the distance as we leave the harbour in Bequia, so navigation is simple. With the northeast trades blowing hard we make good time, and it doesn't take long for the distant shape to resolve itself into a line of scrubby green hills underscored with perfect white beaches.

We anchor in Charleston Bay – a wide open expanse of beautiful turquoise water surrounded by low hills. Surprisingly, given the crowds at Bequia, there's hardly anyone else here. The beaches north of the township are stunning and we take the dinghy to explore them. Skimming over the flat water, a big barracuda leaps clear of the surface in front of us, almost landing in our inflatable. Whilst snorkelling off one of these beaches a grey shape materialises to my left, and I find I'm swimming with a reef shark that's cruising the shallows inshore of me. It takes no notice of me, intent on nosing its way around the coral heads. Unfortunately, as we have seen elsewhere, while there's plenty of sea life, the coral seems to be dead or dying. There are no coloured corals, instead a wasteland of grey decaying reef interspersed with some intricate fan structures and the occasional crinkled knob of brain coral.

We stay here for two nights – the second being New Year's Eve. There's lots of discussion about what we should do to celebrate the conclusion of 2022 and RL goes ashore to reconnoitre, coming back with elaborate plans. In the end we have dinner on the boat before heading to Soho House, a flash resort on the beach, for drinks. There's a band playing covers of Bob Marley; we listen to it for a while, but there's not much life so we cross to the Conch Bar on the other side of the island. The drinks are cheaper here, and we sit on a low wall watching the gentle swell tumble and break across a beach made from thousands of conch shells, their shiny pink interiors glinting in the moonlight. Later we squeeze into a shared minicab for the short drive back to Soho House; it has now thrown its doors open to all comers and is packed. Once midnight is safely behind us, Til and I sneak back to the boat leaving RL, Kate and Alfie partying the night away.

New England cottage: watercolour by Matilda Dumas.

In the marina at Wickford Cove.

Kent at the helm going through NY.

Thomas catches a wahoo.

Approaching the Pitons.

El Oro: acrylic on board by Matilda Dumas.

RL and Randel.

Jason preparing a mahi mahi.

Approaching the anchorage at night: watercolour by Matilda Dumas.

Mid Atlantic rescue.

Anchorage in Flores.

Leafy repairing the ensign.

Philip strapped into the galley.

El Oro in Flores.
Photo: Mia Frayne.

Fiskardo.

Anchored next to Four Seasons in Paxos.

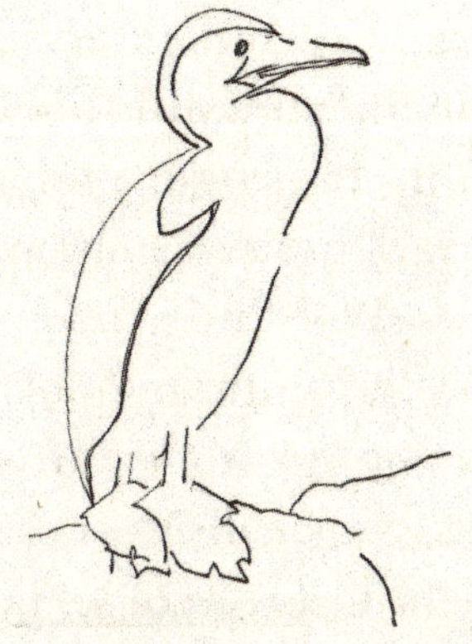

JANUARY

JANUARY 1 IS A BIT SLOW. It kicks off with RL taking the dinghy back to Soho House to pay his bill for the previous evening. After a few cups of coffee and some Panadol, we up anchor and head a little further southwest for Mayreau. This is a tiny but charming island adjacent to the Tobago Cays. It's late afternoon when we anchor in Saline Bay, and in the last of the daylight we walk up the steep hill to the old church founded by a Dominican Monk, Father Divonne, who built much of the infrastructure on the island. The church is on the highest point, and we lean over the fence looking out towards the Cays in the distance, a vast panorama of coral reefs stretching to the horizon, passages of darker blue water indicating the channels between them.

Next morning, we motor the short distance to the Tobago

Cays taking the southern route through the reef. We've read up about the wonder of this place and our expectations are high. It's breathtakingly beautiful, the coral showing up in shades of yellow and green, contrasting against the sapphire-coloured deeper water. Unfortunately, we're not the only ones drawn to this place, and we find ourselves heading towards a forest of masts. There are hundreds of boats here, some on anchors but mainly moored, and it's a small area. Some are in the shelter behind the small islets that make up the Cays, but others anchor behind the reef, exposed to the full force of the wind.

Turtles surface to the right and left of us. Lifting their scaly heads, they stay briefly on the surface, rolling in the messy chop before diving under the waves. Although the water is crystal clear it's impossible to make out the turtles once they dive as they look exactly like rocks on the seabed. We anchor back from the crowds, tucked behind Petit Rameau but next to some enormous vessels –Wylde Swan, a square rigger from the Netherlands taking a group of teenagers on a sail training adventure and Mes Amis, a 144M yacht which can be chartered for upwards of €150K per week. Later a huge 5 masted square rigger comes in and joins our crowd.

We take the inflatable and run round to the windward side of Petit Rameau, getting soaked as we drive into the choppy wavelets. Til, Alfie and I try snorkelling along Horseshoe Reef. The wind blows straight over the top of the reef and we're waterboarded as the waves spill over the top of our snorkels. The dinghy anchor won't hold in the strong wind, so we change plan, going ashore and explore some of the small islands. The heat of the sun is pleasant as we follow pathways through thorny bush, out of the wind. As the sun sets, we're back on board, sitting in the cockpit and half a mile to our north, we see a charter yacht run directly onto the reef. One moment it's reaching with all sails up and the next it lurches to a halt, stuck fast. Several small local motorboats go to help; they take a line from the top of the mast and heel the boat right over before dragging it off. We're too far to hear the sound but can imagine the crunch as the keel drags over the coral.

Next morning, we head back through the reef and a few miles south to Palm Island, a beautiful lunchtime anchorage. It's the picture-perfect Caribbean Island; dazzling white sandy beaches, palm trees and aquamarine water but it's also a private and unfriendly resort. We get ticked off for not wearing shoes in the outdoor bar and again for swimming in the wrong spot. We don't linger, moving half a mile across the channel to Union Island where we anchor in Clifton Harbour. Unusually this anchorage is on the windward side of the island exposed to the trades but sheltered behind a long finger of coral.

Union Island is charming and shambolic. The island is striking with high jagged hills along the interior and a handful of ramshackle villages fringing the coast. It's the southernmost point of our journey this time around and we can't stay long as we need to get Alfie back to Martinique to catch a flight out. At the customs post there's a scrum of people jostling to try and get to the desk, and it takes a long time before we get processed. An angry South African superyacht skipper complains loudly he's paid a lot of money for an expedited check out, but no one pays him much attention.

Once we eventually get the exit stamps in our passports we nose back out around the fringing reef and, hoisting all sail, head north once again. With the north-easterly breeze, we're slightly off the wind and we sail fast in flat water through the Grenadines. Dusk sees us off Bequia and we push on into the night. The passage to St Vincent is rough and a current takes us off to the west. We reef the main and soon afterwards the sheath on the genoa halyard gives way, so we roll that in and replace it with the staysail. It's a timely move as the night is punctuated with rain squalls that also bring a lot of wind. One of these is so strong the rain flattens the water, huge drops pounding the surface. The deluge is so intense it is impossible to look forward. Fortunately, it passes quickly but Alfie and I on watch are drenched.

The passage between St Vincent and St Lucia is even rougher and by now we are hard on the wind. Water cascades into the dorade vents which we haven't properly sealed off, soaking the bunks below. Once behind St Lucia the wind drops off, but the sea is lumpy and confused and it's impossible to motor faster than 4 knots. It's also fluky and the squalls bring 30-degree shifts that are hard to negotiate. Around 8.00am we make our way into Rodney Bay and drop anchor exhausted. It's been a tougher sail than we'd anticipated, and a good learning experience for me. I've pushed the crew harder than I should have. They're not professional sailors, they're on holidays. Kate makes it clear she doesn't want to do any more night sailing.

Next day we make the crossing to Martinique. It's windy and rough, the northeast trades have a lot of north in them, so we make slow progress to Le Marin where we eventually anchor next to some buoys that look suspiciously like they're marking a sunken yacht. From here, after stocking up at the boulangerie, it's an easier sail with the wind behind us along the coast to Fort de France. We pull out the genoa and staysail and have them goosewinged as El Oro surges through the building seaway. We sail inside Diamond Rock marvelling how British troops could possibly have dragged cannons to the top of the vertiginous cliffs. The story goes the British redcoats blockaded the French by occupying the rock which is a mile from the Martinique coast. The French were unable to dislodge them until someone came up with the idea of wrecking a ship's boat filled with rum at the base of the rock. The British defenders became so drunk they were unable to resist the French attack and the rock was liberated.

We track around the southwest corner and cruise north past some interesting looking anchorages which we note for future visits, and into the large inlet that leads to Fort de France. There are several ships anchored off the port and some confusing sandbars to keep us concentrating. We want to anchor off the town centre but are put off by the boats there rolling to the south westerly swell and instead we cross back across the inlet to Anse Miton for a very comfortable night. Kate and RL go ashore in the dinghy with Alfie looking for some party action but come back reporting there are a few beach houses, but nothing else of interest.

After an uneventful night we cross back to Fort de France centre ville and go ashore but it's a Sunday and everything is shut including the customs office so we can't check out ahead of leaving the next morning. Later we motor up to the head of the inlet and anchor in a secluded bay off the end of the airport. We drop the dinghy in and head ashore with Alfie to meet his plane. There's a small boatyard called Port Cohe. It's a tiny inlet surrounded by mangroves and is used as a hurricane hole. It looks like several yachts must have sheltered there in previous storms and been abandoned when they became damaged as we pass waterlogged hulls coated in weed and barnacles. There are a few other smaller sailing yachts and motorboats, but the place is deserted, and it's creepy. We tie our dinghy up to a decrepit wharf, stepping cautiously in case the boards give way. From there we emerge through the scrub next to the runway and walk a mile to the terminal building to farewell Alfie. He's excited to be heading back home to start his new life at university. We're sad to see him go.

While at the airport I try and contact the customs to see if we can check out as we want to leave early the next morning. It's tricky as I have to speak to them in pidgin French through an intercom as they won't emerge in person. The upshot however is we can't, we'll have to clear out in the town. I google the customs office and see it's close to where we're moored, so in the early morning I zip over in the dinghy to the other side of the cove. There's a rough landing spot – a muddy track with a few old hulks dragged ashore. I tie up to a palm tree and walk up the track to emerge in a modern business park. The customs office is easy to find, and I approach an overweight Frenchman smoking at his desk. Again, the answer to my request to clear out is 'non'. There is some gesticulating and I get the gist that yachts must clear out at the facility in the town centre. His office is for ships. So, it's back to the centre ville once more. Eventually we locate the right spot, and from there the process is straightforward.

There's a helpful southerly breeze pushing us along as we hug the coast. We pass Saint Pierre, devastated by the catastrophic volcanic eruption in 1902 which killed 30,000 people. There are about a dozen wrecks marked on the chart off the town beach, victims of the eruption. The breeze swings round to the east and strengthens as we cross the strait to Dominica. We make short work of the 20-mile passage of open water and by mid-afternoon we are in the lee of Dominica. Lush green peaks shrouded in cloud sweep down to the water. There's a cruise ship moored off Roseau but little other shipping. The breeze swings behind us and we take advantage of it, pushing on to Portsmouth at the northern end of the island even though we know this will mean anchoring in the dark. Predictably, once we make this decision the wind promptly drops – however now mentally committed, we turn the engines on and motor through the fading light. It's pitch black when we get to Prince Rupert Bay; there's no moon and clouds have covered the stars, so we have the radar on to avoid unlit boats. It looks like the bay is empty at first, but when we get closer, we see a mass of red dots on the radar, like an outbreak of measles revealing multiple anchored yachts.

It's hard to spot anchor lights against the township behind, but we pick them out as we come up to the silent dark shapes. I have a moment of panic coming into the moored boats as the boat doesn't respond when I turn the wheel. It takes a few seconds before I work out what's happening; I've left the autohelm on. Fortunately, we miss everyone, and I have the steering back by the time we drop our anchor in a tight gap. It's a relief to turn the engines off and relax with a stiff drink. It has been a long day.

We keep going in the morning as we are trying to get to Antigua in time to meet Kate and RL's son Jackson and his girlfriend Lucie. The crossing to Guadeloupe is uneventful and we track through the middle of Les Saintes, the seas crashing spectacularly against jagged rocks, a small fishing boat bobbing perilously close to the foaming white water. From there we cross the six-mile gap to the main island and follow the long coastline north. Like Dominica the island is high and thickly vegetated although there is a strip of ribbon development right along the coast. There aren't many good anchorages on the west coast, and we take shelter for the night in a deep but narrow cove midway along the island called Anse a la Barque. There's space for a couple of yachts but we don't have much room to swing which is tricky as we're anchored in nearly 15 metres of water and have plenty of chain out. Fortunately, the breeze dies, and we sit quietly. After dark we play the torch over the water and see large shapes moving under the boat. We speculate they could be sharks, but we can't make them out clearly.

From here we push on directly to Antigua. It's about 50 miles away and we should comfortably be able to make this in the daylight. The breeze falls light, and we motor much of the way arriving in English Harbour late afternoon in a shower of rain. Freemans Bay, the anchorage at English Harbour is crowded and we slip in behind a wooden yawl manned by a cantankerous single hander. He growls at us we're too close and will swing into him, but he calms down when we tell him we won't be there for long.

I take the dinghy ashore to Nelson's dockyard and go through the usual protracted check in process. It involves going to separate offices for health clearance before going on to customs and immigration. It's pouring with rain and by the time I get to the customs building, the forms the health officer has given me have become a soggy paper mâché mess.

Once cleared in, we go round to neighbouring Falmouth, to the relief of our single-handed neighbour and find better shelter. Falmouth is a great anchorage and much easier to access than English Harbour. You follow the channel in, zig zagging around the reef into a large, sheltered bay with plenty of space. The small town is at the head of the bay and there are also a couple of sandy beaches, easy to get to in the dinghy. From the town it's a short walk over the isthmus back to English Harbour.

Jackson and Lucie arrive the next day and we are now six on board. Thinking they might want to see some typical Caribbean scenery we motor around to Nonsuch Bay on the eastern tip of the island. It turns out not to be such a great idea as although it's only seven miles from Falmouth it's directly upwind and we motor into a short steep chop. The engines struggle to make much progress through the seaway, and it takes a long time. The motion is horrible and it's not long before Lucie is feeling sick. The uncomfortable journey is mitigated somewhat by the beautiful anchorage in aquamarine water, and we spend a relaxing afternoon swimming and snorkelling.

Juggling people coming and going onboard is difficult and at times we feel like travel agents. It's also difficult to keep everyone happy. We agreed with RL to pick up Jackson and Lucie from Antigua because it was the cheapest place for them to fly into. Having worked our way there from St Lucia, around 200 nautical miles to the south, we now realise we've underestimated some of the distances in the Caribbean and left ourselves a long slog up and down the chain of islands. We need to be back in St Lucia in a few days to pick up Evie and in a fortnight be back in Antigua to drop off Jackson and Lucie as well as pick up Jai, Evie's boyfriend. Kate is adamant we shouldn't sail at night which makes for a lot of very long days sailing.

We plan to leave at first light but when the dawn comes, we're enveloped in a thick band of rain with gusty blasts of wind. When the rain eases, I make the decision to leave, but it turns out to be the wrong call. We're still motoring out of the gap in the reef and hauling up the heavy mainsail when we get hit by a second more powerful squall. Visibility drops to zero with driving rain and spray and we urgently pull the main back down trying to secure the flogging sail to the boom. I'm steering by the GPS through a narrow and winding channel, and I try to shut out the thought that if the engine goes, we'll be on the coral in a moment.

We make it out unscathed and in time the rain clears, and we hoist the sails. Unfortunately, the northeast trades have turned south easterly so what should have been a comfortable broad reach is now a beat. We dodge rain squalls all the way across the 40-mile channel to Guadeloupe furling in the huge genoa, a three-man job, every time one gets close. The crossing takes most of the day and in the evening, we motor along the coast eventually anchoring off Pigeon Beach a little to the south of our anchorage when we came the other way.

As we're on a mission to get south, we leave early the next day heading to Dominica. There are a few mutterings about this not being a holiday, but we need to keep moving if we're going to get to St Lucia in time to meet Evie. The breeze still has a some south in it which is frustrating, but it's light and the sea is flat behind the island, so we make good progress motor sailing. I suggest we shake out the reef but get some pushback from Kate who has been shaken by the squally sail the day before, so we leave it in.

In the afternoon we see a pod of pilot whales. At first, we mistake them for dolphins; they look similar albeit larger, but they're sitting motionless in the water. Later that afternoon, after we've crossed over to Dominica, we come across two sperm whales. We spot their spume ahead of us and put the engine into neutral and glide over to them. They are floating under the surface, the top of their backs out of the water. As we approach, one dives slowly beneath us. Its blue grey skin is wrinkled and worn like an old leather jacket and as it dives it turns and looks up at us, its eye clearly visible as it sinks into the clear blue water. Much later I hear a report on the radio that Dominica is a favourite gathering place for sperm whales. So much so that a centre has been established to record their language, a distinct series of clicks, with a view to using AI to try and decode it. Perhaps one day we'll be able to speak to these mysterious creatures.

By evening we're off Roseau and we try to find an anchorage. The land onshore is steep, and the slope continues underwater making it hard to find a safe place to stop. There are some moorings, but we're a heavy boat and I don't trust them. We eventually find a very narrow shelf close to the shore, but it doesn't leave us much room to swing and although we end up dropping the hook, I'm not happy with where we are.

There's also some dissention among the crew. Kate tells

us Lucie is unhappy and not enjoying the voyage. It's not the holiday she anticipated, and she would prefer to be spending more time on the beach. When we ask Lucie about this, she denies it. It seems it's Kate who is unhappy, she has found a lot of the sailing stressful and frightening. She is also trying to ensure the best possible experience for Lucie and Jackson. Things aren't helped when I insist we push on that night. We have dinner at anchor but I'm not comfortable with the anchorage and it's a beautiful calm night, so it makes more sense to keep going to Martinique. Kate is vehemently against this and there are some harsh words spoken.

I end up overruling her and we leave at 10.30pm after dinner and a couple of hours rest. It's a perfect moonlit night with the breeze on the beam at about 10kts. RL and Kate take first watch and motor sail with the main, mizzen and staysail. When I suggest they roll out the genoa and turn off the engine, Kate's not keen, so we leave it until we come up for our watch at 2.00am to unfurl the large headsail and finally there's silence as we switch both engines off. The seas are smooth and the sky a patchwork of golden pinpricks as we glide through the darkness. At dawn we're south of Saint-Pierre and we carry our sail all the way around the corner to Fort de France arriving there at breakfast time.

We do a big stock up shop in the good French supermarkets and motor across to Anse Noir on the southern shore of Fort de France Bay. There are two deep inlets side by side and Anse Noir is the northern one. There are a few French holidaymakers relaxing on the beach and kids are jumping off the jetty. Both bays are fringed with rocks and low cliffs with some interesting caves which we explore by dinghy. It's overcast but the water's clear and the snorkelling is excellent. Here for the first time, we find colourful live coral and beautiful sea fans swaying gently in the current. We also take the opportunity to have a good talk about the tensions on board. We don't fully resolve things but after some discussion we agree to change the itinerary, so we no longer need to go back to Antigua. This means changing Jai's flight as well as Lucie and Jackson's, so they fly out of St Lucia. It's expensive and a little frustrating as it limits our opportunity to explore some of the Leeward Islands – but it does diffuse the situation.

We are also worrying about the anchor winch again. The mechanism has been working well since the repair but the housing which Chinaman welded up has some play in it. When we lift the anchor the whole windlass swivels through ten degrees, and it must be close to breaking free from the deck altogether. We get into the anchor locker and strap it up tightly with ratchet straps which stops the movement. It's not going to last forever though, and we chase up Huttons, the Australian winch manufacturer who are supposed to be sending us a replacement part.

We push on to St Lucia the next morning arriving back in Rodney Bay in the late afternoon. It's like coming home as we anchor in our usual spot under the fort. From there we organise with Chinaman to get the pulpit finished. We moor up in a space left by the Pearl which is out on a day cruise. Despite telling us to get there at 8.30 in the morning, Chinaman is working on St Lucian time and doesn't get started on our pulpit until after 2.00pm. He and his team use large blocks of wood to bend the stainless steel into place dropping the blocks on the tubing at strategic spots. It's remarkably effective and he straightens the major bends before using the tubing we bought in Martinique to fashion a new rail. It all takes time however and at nightfall he hasn't finished, and we try to move to our allocated marina berth. We cast off from the wharf and engage gear but go nowhere. The tide has dropped, and we're stuck firmly in the mud. I ramp up the revs on both engines until they're both full forward; our propellors churn up the water behind us but we still don't move. It's going to be awkward when the Pearl returns if we're still in their spot. When we use the dinghy to pull our bow out into deeper water however, we gradually break free of the suction and slide forward. We cross the 50m or so to our pen and are tying up when Evie arrives. Randel has picked her up from the airport.

Chinaman brings his welding kit around to the marina in the morning and he and Claudius finish the job leaving El Oro with a shiny repaired pulpit. They toss the metal offcuts into the water and leave us to work out how to reconnect the navigation lights. The wiring for these runs inside the pulpit tubes and need to be rethreaded and run back into the boat. It's an awkward and fiddly job.

Now we have Evie on board, and we don't have to rush back to Antigua, we can take things easy. We start by returning to Marigot Bay. Strong northerly winds push us in the right direction, and we hug the coast with staysail and mizzen. We anchor in our favourite spot in the entrance to the bay and go into the bar for happy hour.

Next day we push further to Soufriere anchoring off Malgretoute beach. Randel has told us he used to work as a guide on the Pitons when he was younger and we prevail on him to help us get to the top of Petit Piton, a vertical edifice of rock and jungle, shaped like an incisor. We rendezvous with him on the beach and then slog up a steep muddy path through dense bush. The path turns into a dry watercourse strewn with large boulders and the walk becomes a scramble requiring arms as well as legs. We stretch out into a long line, Lucie who's the fittest at the front, the rest of us trailing in her wake. I'm wearing hiking boots, but Randel is making his way up in thongs. Rotten looking ropes have been hung over the more precipitous sections and we use them to pull ourselves up. At some point these are going to give way and I keep a hand on the rock. After a couple of sweaty hours, we emerge from the thick bush into lighter scrub and moments later we're at the top, 2,500 ft above the beach. The view is spectacular; we can make out Vieux Fort at the southern tip of the island and look across to St Vincent twenty miles further on. To the east we can see deep into the wooded interior. On the other side of the Piton, we look down and see El Oro, a tiny speck on a blue carpet far below us. The descent is almost harder than going up and we are sore and stiff by the time we arrive back at the boat.

After a relaxing couple of days, we head north again. There's a fee, payable to the park rangers each night on the moorings around Soufriere so, although it's beautiful, we want to get back to Rodney Bay for some free anchorage time. After a quiet night at anchor, we wake up to no lights on the circuit boards. Nothing electrical works at all. There's no water from the tap, we can't flush the heads, we can't run the fuel pump to start the engines, we're stuck. This is something we haven't come across before and I call Kent, who's in Italy, for advice. He's not sure but has us checking connections and trying to reset the batteries but without any luck. Part of the problem is the boat has been rewired at various times and there are switches to different circuits some of which are redundant but haven't been removed so we spend time toggling useless buttons.

Out of ideas we take the dinghy ashore to try and find some help. Ulrich isn't interested, but there is a small electronics shop at the back of the marina with an expatriate Englishman called Jon White. Jon is friendly but wary and he looks as if he carries the weight of the world on his shoulders. He is also a man in demand; it's peak season in the Caribbean and every yacht in St Lucia with any electrical issue heads to him for help and he's a one-man band. 'I'm doing some big installations right now. I could possibly see you in a couple of weeks…' he says wringing his hands.

We pour out our sob story; we're crippled and can't possibly wait a couple of weeks. He sighs and says, 'if you can get yourselves into the marina I'll try and pop round for five minutes on Monday and have a look.' It's now Friday so we have a couple of days to manage, but it's better than two weeks.

After a lot of mucking around we eventually get one engine going and limp into the marina. Our inverter keeps tripping however and we can't get any 240V power. There's something weird going on as we now find the freshwater tap is working even though the water pump should be powered by the dead 240V circuit. Jackson takes advantage of this to makes us a cup of tea. Til takes one sip and spits it out in disgust. It's salt water! Jackson must have used the wrong tap, an easy mistake to make. Later I taste the water from the freshwater tap and am shocked to find it is indeed salt. I'm starting to think perhaps the boat is possessed.

On Monday, true to his word, Jon calls round and has a look. He diagnoses it's the remote Victron Blue meter tripping the system. This is a power management device that sits on the switchboard. Once we remove this, the power comes back on and freshwater flows from the tap once again. He has a look at our geriatric bank of batteries and shakes his head. 'If it was me, I'd be replacing all this lot,' he says.

FEBRUARY

Jon shows us how to balance our batteries which takes a couple of days connected to shore power. I take the time to fit the new battery monitor we've bought from him. Once that's done, we can see the charge flowing in and out, and all the history is also graphed up so we can see trends and anticipate trouble coming. Best of all, the data can be accessed on my phone via an app so I can lie in my bunk and watch the batteries charging. Like watching paint dry, says Til. From this time on we never again trip the low voltage alarm.

Whilst there we say goodbye to Jackson and Lucie who fly back to London and hello to Jai, Evie's boyfriend who flies in from Sydney. We also have another couple of guests joining us from the US for a brief stay; Karyn and Marty who are old friends of RL. Marty went to school with RL in Melbourne and had a career in the police as part of the Special Operations Group. It must have been an exciting career as Melbourne at that time was plagued with gang warfare and the SOG were on the front line. After twenty years in the police, he emigrated to the US and learned to fly helicopters; a transition he described as costing him his first marriage.

He remarried a bubbly blond American, Karyn who we were quickly informed used to be Miss Michigan, or perhaps it was Alabama, in the late 80s. Karyn works for a pharmaceutical company and her work seems to have spilled over to her personal life. She has pills for everything and arrives wearing a seasick patch and bands. She also produces a blood pressure monitor from a pouch and checks her blood pressure 3 times a day. We all have fun playing with this machine testing ourselves.

RL hasn't seen Marty since he left Melbourne a lifetime ago and they have a lot to catch up on. We are amused by the disparity in their politics. RL and Kate have a left leaning world view and are always politically correct. On Australia Day they asked if we could take down El Oro's British ensign as they saw it as a symbol of oppression. Marty and Karyn are the opposite end of the spectrum, pro guns and enthusiastic supporters of Donald Trump. Evie finds this fascinating, asking probing policy questions, seeing if she can garner an extremist response. The rest of us make a concerted effort to avoid too much political discussion but it's hard to ignore the differences.

We meander our way back along the coast stopping first at Marigot Bay and on to Soufriere where we anchor for a couple of nights under the Pitons. The weather is perfect and it's a hard spot to beat. The second evening we go round to the resort at Sugar Bay and later Marty produces a bottle of Tequila and he and Karyn drink the contents. Everyone gets quite drunk, but our two new guests are very far gone. At one stage Kate puts a paralytic Karyn to bed but she reappears shortly afterwards. It's dark and we're sitting opposite Karyn and Marty in the cockpit when they start making out in front of us. It begins with them kissing in a long passionate embrace and soon escalates. She slips her bottoms off and straddles Marty and the next thing we know they are going hammer and tongs three feet away from us. RL threatens to throw a bucket of cold water over them, but they ignore him, so we decamp to the foredeck and leave them to it.

In the morning there are a few sore heads, and no one makes any mention of the night-time activities. We head back towards Rodney Bay but haven't gone far when there's a loud bang followed by a clattering sound from the starboard propeller shaft. It sounds as if it's about to shake itself loose. I quickly throttle back and switch off the key before going into the engine room where I lock off the shaft with a pin so it can't move any further. Assuming we must have become tangled in some debris we motor slowly on one engine as far as Marigot Bay. Once there I pull on a mask and snorkel and dive over the side. The port propeller looks normal, so I swim round to the starboard side. To my dismay there are only two blades on the three bladed propeller. I come up for air and go for another look. The three blades meet in a central hub and where the missing blade should be there's a small post with an exposed thread. It looks like the blade has unscrewed itself and dropped off. How could this have happened?

We keep the shaft pinned to minimise any additional vibration and motor back to Rodney Bay. It takes a long time bashing into the stiff breeze with one engine and it's late afternoon before we get there. It's difficult to manoeuvre with one working propeller and we cautiously edge into a pen in the marina.

Our propellers are made by a UK company called Brunton's. They are designed so each blade can pivot separately, and they automatically change pitch to suit the prevailing wind and sea conditions. They are also very expensive. We get onto Brunton's, and they tell us we can't buy a replacement blade, we'll have to either buy three new blades so they can be correctly balanced or alternatively we can buy a whole new propeller. The boat will need to be lifted out of the water to do this work, so it's a big operation.

After a bit more discussion, Brunton's tell us they can produce the new blades in around a week. Producing a whole new propeller will take longer and cost £1,000 more. As luck would have it, we have some friends from the UK, Ivan and Tanya, joining us in around 10 days so potentially they can bring the replacement blades with them. I have another good look at the propeller hub underwater and the stub of shaft from the broken blade is stuck in the thread. I can't see how we're going to get this out and I'm worried if we can't, we won't be able to fit the new blade and we'll need to get a whole new propeller. Nonetheless getting the separate blades bought out to us in just over a week seems worth the risk and we push on with that option.

In the meantime, Marty and Karyn leave us. They've booked into a resort near Castries. They've been with us for four days although it feels much longer. Kate and RL also leave the following day. RL has been on the boat since Rhode Island, almost four long months, and has been an unfaltering support through all sorts of challenges. We would have struggled without his reassuring presence – particularly in the early days after Kent left. Things became more strained later, after Kate joined; she never wanted to be on the boat for so long. We're sad to see them go but we're also very much ready for a change.

Now it's Til and me, Evie and her boyfriend Jai. We leave the marina and anchor out in Rodney Bay happy to relax. Three days later Dominic and Shoonagh join us. They are an English couple who we met years before in Australia; we had small children of similar ages. At the time, we thought them the most incompatible couple. Shoonagh was going through a phase as a born-again Christian whilst enthusiastically supporting a range of left-wing causes, while Dominic worked for a bank and had a much more conservative outlook. They've proved us wrong having thrived together over the years, a good demonstration that opposites attract. Although we live the other side of the world, we've kept in touch, and they are now some of our closest friends.

After saying farewell to Evie and Jai, who are on their way to Brazil, we make plans with Shoonagh and Dominic. They're looking for a change of scenery as they've had an emotionally exhausting few weeks. Shoonagh's mother has died after a long battle with dementia and the funeral was the day before they flew out to St Lucia. We collectively agree we're not going to be constrained by the lack of a propeller and after another night at anchor in Rodney Bay we head across the straits to Martinique. It's a typical crossing, breezy and bumpy and we get across quickly, anchoring in our usual spot in Le Marin.

Once there I run the generator; alarming clouds of white smoke billowing out of the exhaust. We have Nigel Calder's 'Boatowners Mechanical & Electrical Manual' on board which is the bible. I thumb through the index until I get to white smoke and the gist seems to be it's either unburned diesel – very bad, or it's steam – still not good, but should be fixable. I put my hand over the exhaust and the 'white smoke' seems to condense into water so it should be steam. That's a relief, so it's back to the manual as well as to YouTube which has me checking for blockages in the raw water system. After some fruitless searching and much head scratching, I check the rubber impeller and sure enough it turns out to be missing most of its blades. It's a battle to replace and I end up removing the water pump to get to it, but it's a satisfying moment when I try the generator again and it runs with no steam.

As I'm on a repair drive, I also fit the new Victron Cerbo which keeps track of our inverter as well as the batteries. We'd ordered this from Jon to replace the faulty Victron remote monitor which was tripping the inverter. I was a bit wary about whether I'd be able to fit this electronic gadget myself, but Jon reassured me it was simple, and it turns out to be so. The hardest part is laying the cables from one side of the boat to the other under the various floorboards and lockers. Whilst on a roll I also tackle the coffee machine which has died again. It's fiddly to take apart and I've been putting it off, but now more confident after my recent successes, I spend the morning pulling the machine to bits and removing all traces of coffee debris before reassembling it. Miraculously it springs back into life, and we enjoy a round of cappuccinos.

After celebrating all this success, we decide to move anchorages to the more scenic St Anne's around the corner. It's blowing hard and with one engine it's difficult to retrieve the anchor without any strain on the windlass. Til's up at the bow and has most of the chain up when the windlass starts slipping before losing all traction. She waves at me and shouts something I can't hear in the wind, and I run forward to see the chain rattling back out into the sea. For a moment it looks like we're going to lose it all overboard; I can't recall if the end of the chain is attached to the boat. Fortunately, the movement slows, and we manage to grab the heavy galvanised links and cleat it off. I take the windlass apart and am horrified to discover the pawl carrier that goes around the shaft has sheared in two. This is a critical part of the mechanism that connects the drive shaft to the drum of the winch. It's a circle of metal made from bronze and linked to the shaft by a small metal key. Somehow this key has rolled out of its slot and caused the carrier to shear.

The upshot is the shaft turns, but the winch itself doesn't. Once again, we don't have a working windlass in addition to having one working propeller.

The good news is this latest drama has happened in Martinique; it's a major yachting hub, so we may be able to get some help. Leaving Dominic and Til on board to mind the boat, Shoonagh and I fire up the outboard and head ashore. The winch is a Hutton, designed and produced in Australia so it's unlikely we'll find a replacement part, but we might be able to find someone who can machine up an alternative. We spend the morning trawling around a series of chandleries and machinist shops. Fluent in French and stubbornly tenacious Shoonagh relishes the challenge of trying to get us going once again. Mostly we receive Gallic shrugs and uninterested 'non's. Shoonagh won't take no for an answer, pushing reluctant shopkeepers to give us some suggestions where we can try next. Eventually we are passed onto Caraibe Metal, a sprawling warehouse on the edge of the main shipyard and across from the enormous travel lift which can lift out boats up to 400 tonnes. Here we meet Pierre Loic, an expatriate Frenchman who tells us to call him Pilow. Diminutive in stature with a set of broken brown teeth and a twinkle in his eye he's outside smoking and deeply engaged in conversation when we meet him. He waves away our advances, and we wait politely to one side until he's free, expecting a swift rejection to our query. When he eventually finishes his conversation and stubs out his gauloise, he ushers us up a rickety set of stairs to a mezzanine level above a warehouse and into his office. He gestures vaguely at some chairs covered in files and paper and after some reorganisation we sit across his desk. The conversation becomes animated, and I struggle to follow. Shoonagh refers to google translate occasionally to clarify some nautical term but otherwise holds sway confidently. The upshot is it's hard to get bronze cast in Martinique. He could get the part replicated in stainless steel, but it would be difficult, and it wouldn't be a long-term solution as it's the wrong metal. It would be better if we can find the right part in France from where we can courier it to Martinique via his office. He identifies a potential supplier via google, tells us to note the details and we are waved out of the door.

Back at the boat we do some more on-line research and get in touch with Huttons in Australia. They don't have the part we need on hand; however, it turns out the business in France that Pilow has suggested is a distributor for Hutton. Strangely, they are based in the foothills of the Alps, miles from the nearest water, but after some toing and froing, we are pleasantly surprised when they tell us they have the requisite part and can indeed despatch it to Martinique. We give them Pilow's contact details.

In the meantime, we need to get Dominic and Shoonagh back to St Lucia so they can catch their flights home. This means re-instigating our earlier method of pulling up the anchor manually, taking a line with a hook back to the winch on the mast and bringing in around six metres of chain at a time. To make things more complicated, the trade winds are blowing hard and 25kt bullets are scudding across our exposed anchorage. Til's on the wheel trying to motor slowly forward against the wind, I manage the line on the anchor chain and Dominic and Shoonagh operate the winch on the mast. We get a few overriding turns on the winch and it's slow going but gradually the chain comes up. There are a few nervous moments when the anchor breaks free from the mud and the wind catches us; Til guns our one engine and it takes a few seconds before we get enough momentum to avoid being blown onto the reef to leeward.

Once safely underway we relax and enjoy a boisterous broad

reach back across the Martinique sound and then on south to Soufriere. It's late afternoon by the time we arrive in the bay and we're fortunate to be able to pick up the last remaining mooring. Two boys come past in a dinghy and one of them introduces himself as Ethan and offers to bring us some fish. 'Is it fresh?' asks Til.

'Yes, yes, very fresh. My father will catch it tonight, I'll bring it in the morning,' he replies.

He appears as promised soon after breakfast, proffering a bag with tuna steaks. We pay him and only later when Til goes to prepare the fish, she finds it still frozen.

We spend a couple of idyllic days in the deep clear waters of Soufriere Bay, venturing round the corner to luxurious Sugar Bay before it's time to get back north again. The day before leaving we pick up Randel who we haven't seen for a few weeks. He seems depressed having split up from his girlfriend. He tells me he feels someone has used a witch doctor to put a hex on him. When I express surprise, he shakes his head saying it happens a lot. He relates a story about two fisherman who were out at sea in their open boat off the southern coast of St Lucia when their outboard fails. They were swept far to the west by the trade winds and ended up drifting with no food or water for nearly three weeks. Eventually a fishing boat from Venezuela spots them, but by this stage one of the fishermen has died and the other was very weak. 'That's awful' I exclaim, 'but what has that got to do with witch doctors?'

Randel gives a slight roll of the eyes as if to suggest I am slow catching on. He explains that the man who died was previously involved in an accident resulting in the death of a child. The child's mother would have paid for a witch doctor to arrange for the man's death at sea. Apparently, there's a thriving business among witch doctors in St Lucia. They go to Haiti for training and when they come back can earn good money as people pay them for spells. It's not simply arranging for people's untimely deaths, but you can pay a witch doctor to ruin a relationship or damage a career of an enemy.

'But who would want to do that you?' I ask. He shrugs and shuffles gloomily off to the focsle.

It's a long slow motor against the wind back up to Rodney Bay. With one propeller it takes us a good six hours to complete the 18 miles. Once there, we anchor for a night in the bay, a sign of our growing confidence in our ability to handle the anchor manually. To prove us wrong, the anchor drags the first time, so we bring it up again and reset it with a lot of swearing and cursing. Randel mutters loudly that in all his time on El Oro, nobody has ever deployed the anchor without the windlass working.

The following day Dominic and Shoonagh fly out and we take a marina berth. For once we aren't in our usual place in the pariah J dock but instead on the hammerhead around the more crowded southern side of the marina. I'm worried about our ability to get in with one engine and a strong breeze, but we glide in without difficulty and hand our lines to Nigel, the dockmaster.

After a quick change of bedding and liberal use of the spray vinegar bottle, we're ready for our next guests who come in that same evening. First Ivan and Tanya who come bearing our replacement propeller blades from Brunton's, and a significant excess baggage charge. They're followed an hour or two later by an old friend of Til's, Kirsty, aka the Jester.

Our options where we can go are limited given the constraints on anchoring as well as having only one engine. Ivan and Tanya are not experienced sailors and Tanya has recently undergone a double hip replacement, so we're keen to try and keep things as calm as possible. With that in mind we make for the familiar waters off Soufriere once more. In preparation for the trip, we hoist the dinghy up onto the davits before leaving. When we cast off, the wind twists us round so we're sitting sideways across the narrow channel and try as I might, I can't turn the boat with the one engine. The wind pushes us towards the mangroves and so I motor back towards the pontoon. The same thing happens three or four times, but I can't manoeuvre the boat around the corner to head out towards the open water. While this is happening, several small motorboats weave their way around us as we're blocking most of the channel, but no one offers to try and assist.

In desperation I ask Randel to get the dinghy back in the water. He nods assent but continues to finish texting on his phone. I grit my teeth and try to stay calm as he takes his time on the phone and leisurely unlashes the dinghy and lowers it to the water using the crane. From there he hops in and pulls the starter cord and uses the power of the outboard to push our nose around the corner.

Back at Soufriere the rangers come as usual every night to claim the 54EC mooring fee. In the gloaming they hang onto our rail, and we have a bit of a chat. We're here so often, we're getting to know them. There is a bit of swell coming into the bay and the anchorage becomes rolly. Tanya turns a sickly shade of green and retires to her cabin with a bucket 'just in case'. This is the first time we've had someone get seasick on a mooring; it doesn't bode well if we want to go anywhere more ambitious. The next morning she's still a bit queasy so we give her a Scopoderm patch which seems to help.

Ivan announces we ought to walk up the Pitons, so I prevail on Randel to act as guide once again. We meet him at the small hut at the base of the walk looking gloomily at the sky. It's overcast and intermittent squalls of light drizzly rain have been passing through since before dawn and the path is wet and slippery. Nevertheless, the three of us get going on the long scramble up the steep slope. We trudge in silence focussed on putting one step in front of the other, grabbing onto a tree root or branch for support. The slope is relentless, it's muggy and exhausting. I'm also acutely aware Ivan has recovered from a major heart attack in the not too distant past and the huffing and groaning noises coming from him are far from reassuring. The combination of pouring sweat and persistent drizzle mean his glasses won't stay on so he is also struggling up blind. Periodically a loud curse indicates he's accidentally grabbed hold of a cactus stem for support than a smooth tree trunk. Eventually we emerge from the canopy and the weather clears for us as we reach the summit. Far below us, the sea stretches out as a distant tablecloth of rippled blue satin.

Randel seems lost in gloomy contemplation. He tells me he's depressed about the state of his country. It was a public holiday the day before to celebrate Independence Day and this was accompanied by a violent spate of shootings leaving six people dead. The country is awash with guns and there are rival gangs happy to take any opportunity to settle scores. We were in town the day before and noticed the atmosphere change from friendly celebration to something more intense and intimidating. Til and Jester were standing in a petrol station near the seafront when a long parade of motorbikes came past. They took some footage of the parade, videoing the bikers with bandanas and painted emblems of gang loyalty as well as capturing the ear-splitting roar of their machines. We later discover that twenty minutes after the girls left to return to the boat, two people were shot dead in the very same garage forecourt.

The rest of the week is uneventful. We remain moored in Soufriere for five days and spend our time paddleboarding, swimming or taking excursions ashore. Finally, we pick up Randel once more and head back up to Rodney Bay this time taking a marina berth in the easier to access J Dock. Ivan and Tanya leave us, but Jester extends her trip for another week, pushing back her flight.

The next day, 27 Feb, is booked for the haul out. Randel and I prep the boat, removing both forestays, so we can fit the boat properly into the travel lift. Once the dock is clear, we motor in and wait long beyond our allotted time before the haul out team in faded blue overalls finally come to attend to us. There is a lot of discussion around where the slings should go to avoid damaging the propeller shafts. This is a best guess as I don't have an accurate plan of the boat's underwater layout. We stick blue tape on the hull to mark where we think they should sit. The crane trundles back out over the water, its giant wheels staying within the guide rails. The slings are dropped to the seafloor to go under the keel and once in position, gently tightened. The operator pulls the lever on the lift to take up the slack and the boat rises out of the water. All sets of eyes are on the waterline making sure our assumptions are correct and we're not supporting 40 tonnes of boat on a propeller shaft.

She comes up slowly, black underbelly swollen and dripping. The giant lift rolls back onto the hardstand, with El Oro swaying in the slings. Fortunately, there are no boats waiting behind us, so we are free to hang there for a few hours.

I go and summon Chinaman who has forgotten I'd booked him to come and help. He saunters across along with his young assistant, trademark Glock pistol tucked prominently in his jeans. 'Get me a 22mm socket and a hammer,' he instructs, and the assistant goes scurrying off back to the workshop. We have most of the tools to hand and Chinaman removes the broken propeller without difficulty. He takes it across to his workshop where he welds new metal to the broken thread, stuck deep within the hub. He builds up this piece of metal until it is sticking proud and bonds a long piece of aluminium to it so he can now unscrew it like a giant wingnut. The technique is effective, and the broken piece comes out with little resistance. From there we collectively pour over the instructions from Brunton's and reassemble the propeller with the new blades. There are a series of bearings and locknuts and there is considerable debate about which way around a certain part should go. The instructions suggest one way whilst logic suggests the other way would be more effective. Eventually we settle on ignoring the instructions. Chinaman applies a dose of glue to ensure nothing shifts once it is all sealed as well as a healthy packing of grease.

Our windlass component from France has arrived in Martinique according to the advice on the Chronopost tracker. I've made half-hearted enquiries about getting it couriered to St Lucia, but it all seems a bit difficult to arrange. It's easier for us to go in person to pick it up, especially as we have Jester and Randel on board to help with the manual anchoring. It also means Jester can have a bit of a sail on El Oro as her trip to date has largely involved sitting on a mooring off Soufriere.

Once across the straits we anchor in our usual place at Le Marin well outside the dense cluster of boats. Jester comes with me to find Pilow at Cariabe Metal and if he's surprised to see me accompanied by a different blonde, he doesn't show it. He's all smiles and we are again ushered into the messy office and given a seat as he digs through his piles of paperwork to find a small box. He produces a Stanley knife with a flourish and after a few cuts pulls out a shiny new pawl carrier as well as tiny replacement metal key. Back on board it takes a little bit of filing, but with some persuasion I'm able to slot it over the shaft and our windlass is back in action. After the challenges of the last month, it's a great relief to have two working propellers and a functioning anchor winch.

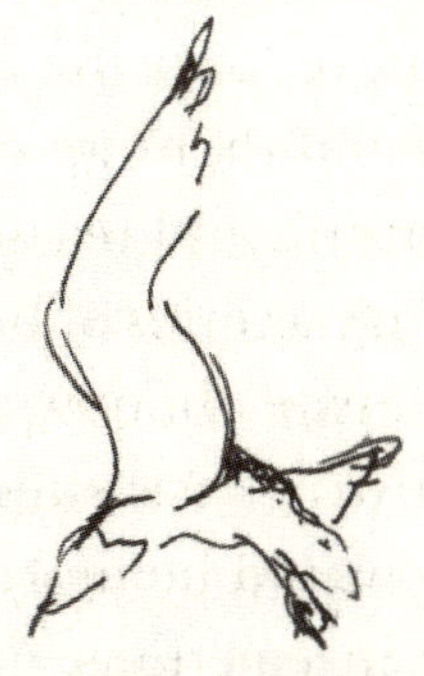

MARCH

We spend a night in Martinique before heading back to the marina at Rodney Bay to meet the six pack. Six Australian mates are coming on board for a month. Jason and Lorna have packed up their lives in Sydney and are on their way to try and buy a boat in Europe. They're accompanied by Nick and Steph and Garry and Alyssa who are all friends from when we lived in Avalon in the Northern Beaches of Sydney. They've all taken a month's holiday to join us in the Caribbean. They arrive the following evening, Jason with mountains of luggage and a kiteboard. Fortunately, we no longer have Randel on board, so we have the forepeak to stow all the excess gear.

The next day finds us contorted in the anchor locker, stuffing around with the windlass once again. Hutton's finally made a new mounting collar and Jason has bought it out for us. The old one, welded together by Chinaman, is very worn and we have the windlass strapped up to prevent it shearing off the deck. We disconnect the windlass and remove it. Last time this was a huge undertaking. Now we know how to do it, it is considerably easier. Unfortunately, it's not all plain sailing as the new collar is the wrong size and doesn't properly fit onto the winch. We go over to see Chinaman and he machines the part on his lathe, so it sits snuggly to the body of the windlass.

Putting the windlass back into the boat, however, proves much more difficult than taking it out. Without pulling equipment it is almost impossible to get the windlass to seat properly up under the deck. We take turns lying on our back in the anchor locker, the chain digging in uncomfortably, trying to force the machine upwards through the deck. The tight space is like a sauna and we're dripping in sweat. Finally, after several hours of effort we manage to get it to stick through the deck enough for the bolts to bite. From there it is a case of gradually tightening them and raising the windlass gearbox, so it fits flush. I'm naively optimistic this is the last work we'll need to do on the windlass.

On our way out of the marina we fill up with fuel and water and from there we take the well-trodden path south to Soufriere for the night. We get going early the next morning and motor through the long wind shadow thrown by the Pitons. Once we're back into the steady trades we raise all sail and make good progress to the south. The breeze is perfect, around 15 knots from the northeast and we surge through the building swell at a comfortable eight knots. In the St Vincent straits Jason tempts fate by flying his drone. It's hard to catch and the landing is stressful. The drone sensors don't like the rigging on the boat, and it is difficult to bring in close. There are no protruding legs to grab hold of and the catchers lined up on deck are wary of the four spinning blades. The landing is messy, the drone bounces on the deck and skids towards the rail before coming to a halt. There's a collective sigh of relief and some muttering from Jason; this will be the last time he flies the drone from a moving boat.

We gradually close the coast of St Vincent, and the verdant interior comes into focus. The highest peak is a volcano, confusingly called La Soufrière; it's still active and recent lava flows have carved brutish scars though the lush vegetation all the way to the beach. The high ground is shrouded in cloud, but the weather remains dry and more importantly the wind holds as we track our way parallel to the shore. By the late afternoon we're close to our destination. The mainsail is hard to pack away with a new crew, but we wrestle it down and motor slowly into Cumberland Bay to be greeted by the local welcoming party. The bay is glassy calm, perfect for paddleboarding and snorkelling and at dusk we pile ashore to the Mojito bar. Later this becomes rowdy as a party of strangely dressed French men take over the bar all sporting pigs' snout appendages strapped to their crotches. We retreat to the boat for dinner.

After a leisurely morning, we untie our stern from the coconut tree and bring up our anchor before motoring south to Bequia. The breeze comes up later and we can sail for a while but it's a short crossing and by lunchtime we're anchored off Princess Margaret beach in Admiralty Bay.

Nobody is in any hurry to go anywhere so we stay a couple of days enjoying the charming situation. There's talk of walking to the other side of the island to see the windward coast but not much action and instead we wander through the town going to the market to stock up on fruit and vegetables before spending the afternoon in one of the many waterfront bars.

When we're ready, we raise the anchor and motor slowly past the long jutting finger of cliffs reaching out to the west. Derelict houses cling to the rocks like abandoned mud nests.

Who lived there and what happened to them? Around the point we turn east, hard onto the breeze and follow the coast past the airport towards the little island of Petit Nevis. We tried to anchor here with RL and Kate a few months before but then it was much too rough. This time the water is calm and even the rocky outcrops off the island look benign. We've read there are the ruins of an old whaling station still used from time to time. It's controversial, but there's an annual whale hunt still practiced in traditional boats and the occasional whale is taken. We've seen whale oil in the markets but haven't tried it. It's hard to imagine the whaling station being used as the ruins are very ruined. There are a few crumbling walls and a derelict concrete wharf. The island is small and it's a short walk across to the windward side and around the cliffs back to where we started from. The water is crystal clear and reveals numerous spiky urchins which make swimming with bare feet hazardous.

After lunch we pull out the big headsail and beat our way east across the short passage to Mustique. This was another place we'd tried and failed to get to during our earlier trip south. The island is beautiful with mansions discretely tucked into the folds of the land. Manicured lawns and tended gardens with palms and white gravel run into perfect sandy coves. We sail past heading for Britannia Bay, the only reasonable anchorage available. There are moorings there and we attempt to pick one up before being shooed off by the harbourmaster. We're too long and too heavy so must anchor and he points vaguely at a spot further along the bay. We drop the hook in 20 metres of water, deeper than I'm happy with, but there's not much wind so we don't worry too much about the holding. We're getting into the dinghy when the harbourmaster reappears. This time he charges us 200EC for the pleasure of anchoring in his bay and tells us we can't walk around the island as it's private, although we can take a taxi tour if we like. Perhaps he's related to the taxi driver.

Ashore it is deathly quiet. Tortoises pick their way along the waterfront, low bellies dragging in the sand, plodding on ungainly limbs. We wander under the manchineel trees. There are signs indicating these are dangerous and not to stand under them in the rain. There are signs marked private and no entry and others indicating picnic tables can be reserved, but not by visiting yachts. It's not very welcoming. Later we hear there have been a few incidents of yachties trespassing on celebrities' privacy. One group hired a golf buggy and drove up Mick Jagger's driveway and were discovered in his swimming pool. It's no wonder they're a bit wary of casual visitors. In the evening we try Basil's bar. The cocktails are good and so is the view, but there's not much of a party. It's expensive and we don't linger.

From Mustique we meander slowly south. It's a short sail to Canouan where once again we anchor in the rolly Charleston Bay. The water is milky blue, the bottom stirred up by unseen currents. We buy some fish from a local in a dinghy. 100EC for 10lb of fish he says holding up two smallish orange reef fish. None of us have any scales to prove him wrong. He fillets them in front of us and the strips of pinkish flesh feed us that evening.

Next day it's on to Mayreau. The anchorage is crowded and there's a swell coming in from the north. We anchor out the back and dinghy into shore. It's hard to land with the surge and you need to time your leap from dinghy to jetty. We find a resort in the afternoon to relax with more cocktails. There are no other guests, it's a mystery how the place can possibly survive. In the morning we risk the shore break once more and head ashore. There's a small steel freighter crashing against the wharf with the surge, pounding against a protective wall of car tyres. A man on the wharf tells us it's on its way back to Guyana. We trudge up the steep path to the top of the hill. It's Sunday and the little church perched on the summit is packed. We hear strains of 'She'll be coming round the mountain when she comes…'. Far below us, the water to the east of the island is clear and blue with the green of the coral leading out to the Tobago Cays.

That afternoon we're there ourselves, anchored once more in the lee of Petit Rameau. We take the dinghy out to the gap through the outer reef and snorkel the wall beyond leading to the blue depths. There's a current flowing and it's a struggle to avoid being pulled out to sea. Back inside the reef we find a shallow sandy area where there are turtles grazing on the sparse seagrass. They take no notice of us as we swim up to them. There are also rays and other translucent fish darting over the sands. Kiteboarders are zigzagging across the shallow waters and Jason is inspired to get his own kite up. It's not windy enough however for his small kite and he comes back a little deflated.

From the Cays we move on again. This time it's the short run to Union Island. The anchorage at Clifton is crowded and we struggle to find a clear space, eventually opting to take a mooring buoy. It's hard to get ashore, it's blocked by a thick layer of sargasso weed that's blown into the bay. It is a rotting barrier between the sea and the land, impossible to motor through. We carve a way through it with paddles. It's hard to imagine how anyone will ever be able to clean this up. The bay is on the exposed, windy side of the island and that evening we head out to the Island Bar, an isolated structure build on foundations of conch shells on top of the protective reef. The place is pumping – full of French charterers who have crossed from Martinique. The drinks are deadly; at first, they seem almost undrinkable but after getting one down the next is easier and the next delicious and by then you are incoherently drunk.

We're sluggish the next morning and we don't leave the island until midday. It turns out to be a public holiday, Heroes' Day, but the immigration office is open, and we check out for Carriacou. It's a few miles to the south so the run doesn't take us long and we anchor off the beach at Hillsborough. There are no other yachts which seems strange. Heading ashore to try and find the customs we tie up to a decrepit wharf which looks like it could fall into the sea at any moment. The town is sleepy with no tourists and the customs show no interest in us at all telling us we'll need to go around the corner to Tyrell Bay.

Late in the day we head around the corner past the beautiful Sandy Island and into a different world. Tyrell Bay is perfectly sheltered and there are hundreds of yachts of all descriptions moored and anchored across the bay. Many have been there for decades, rotting quietly whilst others harbour liveaboards and are clearly more transient.

Checking in as always, proves time consuming. Immigration is done in the yacht marina premises and involves the usual form filling and stamping. The on-line Sailclear system is not working so it's back to carbon paper and handwriting. The customs shed is a dinghy ride away on the other side of the bay as are the port authorities. The whole exercise is a half-day process but eventually we are cleared in and issued a cruising permit for Grenada.

It's about 40 miles to the south of Grenada and the sail takes us across the channel from Carriacou, past the Kick 'em Jenny cluster of islands and down the coast of Grenada itself. We have a boisterous NE breeze pushing us and we surge southwards passing close to the islands. The current kicks up short steep wavelets and we steer oblique to our course to keep on track. Eventually as we get in the lee of the land the wind dies and we motor the last hour or so of the journey to St Georges Bay. We take a berth at Port Louis marina and spend a couple of days relaxing in the comfortable surroundings – most of the crew head off to lie by the pool.

It's interesting exploring St Georges – the politics of the 1980s and the coup leading up to the US invasion are still very much there to see. There's a plaque in the old fort commemorating the people who died, and when we ask, the taxi drivers are quick to tell us about Maurice Bishop the charismatic revolutionary leader who was executed by extremist members of his own regime. In death he's become something of a founding father; there are statues commemorating him and the international airport bears his name.

An arc of green coolant jetting out from a split radiator hose prevents us from leaving. Frustratingly we don't have a spare on board so Jason, Nick and I head into town on the bus to try and find one. The bus system is the same across much of the Caribbean. A series of people movers run frequently to all parts of the island. There's a guy who sits by the sliding side door who operates as the conductor and his role is to squeeze as many people as possible on board as well as take the fare. It's a human jigsaw puzzle as he fits passengers for different destinations into different parts of the vehicle. 'Come on, move up, move up,' he exhorts as Nick, Jason and I are squeezed into the back row of a 12-seat vehicle that already has 18 people packed in. I'm next to a large lady with a shopping bag on her knees, who ignores me as I'm pressed uncomfortably against her. Loud music pumps from the speakers and there's a party atmosphere on board. I've no idea what the fare is, but we proffer a few coins when we get off and we get a high five from the conductor and the bus is gone.

We don't find the exact hose we're looking for, but after visiting several outlets, manage to get some flexible tubing that will suffice. Once that's fitted, we motor sail the short distance to the southwestern corner of the island and from there it's an uncomfortable push against a steep chop to get to the shelter of Prickly Bay, one of a series of fjord like inlets along the southern coast of Grenada.

The bay is lined with nondescript modern houses. It's more like a US suburb than the Caribbean. It's also crowded with moored yachts; the water is murky and there's little to keep us here so next day we head further east. Once again, we battle the wind as soon as we stick our nose offshore, motoring for an hour or so to get to Clarke's Court Bay. The route in is tricky past a set of fringing reefs, waves smashing into the coral sending plumes of spray high into the air. There are fierce bullets of wind, the gusts threatening to push the boat sideways into the waiting coral. It would be another bad place for the engine to fail. We wind around the back of Hog Island and anchor deep in the bay; the waters have narrowed and there is high ground to either side. At the head of the bay there's a desolate boat yard created from an old gravel pit where unloved yachts are propped up on the hardstand, the sand and stones whipped up around them in the wind. No one's around; it's like the end of the earth.

We have a quick beer in Nimrod's rum bar; there's not much there, a few chickens scratching in the dirt and some chairs and tables scattered haphazardly around a small shed doubling as a shop. Some other drinkers tell us about the marina up the road where there will be live music that night. It's called Whisper Cove, and the marina has one small wharf with half a dozen yachts tied up. There's a restaurant and bar above the wharf and as promised, a local yachty is performing covers of a range of 1980s songs. It's another night with way too many cocktails and a scary bill at the end, but we make it back safely to El Oro.

We had planned on spending more time exploring the southern coves of Grenada, but having seen two of them we prefer to make our way north again, taking some time along the way.

We make a couple of hops north back to Carriacou for another night in Tyrell Bay. From there we try a longer sail to Bequia but are put off by the strong NE trades. We are hard on the wind in 25kts and it's uncomfortable and slow and I'm worried about breaking something. After slogging for an hour, we change plans and head for the shelter of Chatham Bay on the west coast of Union Island. We're changing course when there's a loud rattle from the hand line propped over the cleat. A flash of green behind us and shouts of excitement from the crew, we've hooked a fish at last. Jason brings it in hand over hand and a little later we've landed a large mahi mahi. As it hits the deck, the hook falls out of its mouth as it thrashes its way forward. It's close to pushing through the lifelines and safety when Garry wields the rubber mallet and despatches the poor creature. It's a large fish that feeds eight of us for two days: sashimi, followed by steaks and finally fish pie.

The winds ease a little the following day and it's a pleasant sail to windward to get to Bequia. We take care of the formalities, do a bit of shopping and it's on again the next morning. We motor north in the lee of St Vincent trying to make as much distance upwind as we can before hitting the channel. It's a long process and we fill the time by trying to fly the drone once more. To try to make it more retrievable, Jason ties a string below the craft, but this seems to adversely affect the sensors. The drone is high above the boat, but he can't bring it in as the machine sees the string and thinks it is already close to land. There are a nervous few minutes as Jason tries to disable the sensors and eventually brings the machine in, crash landing on the deck. It seems some component is now broken, and drone flying is cancelled for the time being.

Our strategy of getting to windward is effective and we bear away across the strait comfortably able to lay our destination at Soufriere. We smugly watch a stream of catamarans being swept to leeward, although many are headed for Martinique so can afford to come off the breeze a little. A few hours later we're on a mooring in Sugar Bay and it's not long before we're in the bar at the resort for some more overpriced, but delicious cocktails.

In the morning we check in and I take the process a little cheaply running up against the ire of the immigration official. Jason and Nick come ashore with me and buy a case of beer whilst I'm checking in which is strictly not allowed. The immigration officer spots them waiting at the dinghy dock and we are all hauled over the coals for going ashore before being officially approved. The conversation is a little surreal as the official alternates between berating us for our conduct and asking about wine and whether it is good for his health. Eventually we get the stamp however and we're back home in St Lucia.

Back on the boat I take advantage of a quiet moment to service the windlass. I want to check the bolts attaching it to the deck are still tight. I pull off the drum of the winch and to my distress find our new pawl carrier, obtained from France and Martinique with such effort, has sheered in two once again. It seems despite our best efforts the key has rolled again out of its slot and cracked the carrier. My heart sinks as I contemplate the prospect of more weeks ahead without a working windlass.

Via WhatsApp, Kent tells me he's had this problem in the past and when he first took over the boat the windlass was permanent screwed to the driveshaft. He suggests we could look at trying something similar. It's a good idea; we might be able to use a bolt to connect the winch drum directly to the driveshaft. It takes us a while to find the hardened cobalt drill bits we need to bore through the stainless-steel winch and the 50mm shaft. Drilling takes a long time and Garry fashions a lubricating device for the drill tip using washing up liquid and a syringe. We replace the battery on the handheld tool several times before eventually, the deck covered in curly metal shavings, we break through. There's now a hole through the entire apparatus and we knock a long bolt through. It looks like a Frankenstein monster with the bolt through the winch drum and a fat nut on the end, but we've negated the need for the pawl carrier and our windlass works again.

A couple of days later we say goodbye, first to Nick, Steph, Alissa and Garry and later Jason and Lorna. On their last night we're anchored in the bay and in the late afternoon we go ashore for a walk to the fort. Fort Rodney was built to guard the entrance to the bay and it's a short hike up a steep path to the Napoleonic era ruins. On the way back we stop off in one of the beach bars and have a few rum punches. As always these are deadly strong. Back on the boat, we are joined by some German neighbours on a tiny wooden yacht called Holly Golightly. They have recently completed an Atlantic crossing by themselves. The winds were very light, and it took them 26 days from the Canary Islands, which must have been tough. They tell us the story of how one night in the middle of the Atlantic their VHF crackled into life. In front of them was a single-handed rower. A 68-year-old Englishman from the Isle of Wight raising money to support red squirrels. Apparently, he's due to arrive in Rodney Bay in a couple of days.

The Germans come back to El Oro with us, and we have a few more drinks that none of us need. Eight people living on top of each other in a confined space is challenging and there have been a few simmering tensions occasionally threatening to bubble to the surface. Tonight, under the influence of too many rum punches we get a little tired and emotional. The Germans are too polite to mention anything, and we eventually go to bed with hugs and tears all round. It's been an amazing month but we're all ready to move on. We are all close friends who go back a long way, but that somehow makes it harder as we know each other's faults and they occasionally grate.

APRIL

WE'RE LEFT ALONE in the marina where we breathe a sigh of relief and remain for a few days. We're physically and emotionally exhausted. Having eight people on board for a month sailing and partying hard every night is draining, and we're wrung out. It's also the first time we've been properly on our own for months and it feels strange.

The single-handed rower comes into Rodney Bay creating a frisson of excitement. He's a retired stockbroker who looks more like he's stepped out of his office rather than off a tiny boat after months at sea. It's taken him 72 days to do the crossing and he's up for a chat. He has some hair-raising stories about near capsizes and breaking an oar in gigantic waves. He tells us he is not a sailor, in fact knows very little about the sea but made this voyage on a whim.

The neighbouring yacht helps us slip our lines and we motor out and anchor in the bay once more. We're still in recovery mode and happy to do very little for a few days. We spend some time with the Germans on Holly Golightly before they leave on their way to Panama. Eventually, we get our mojo back; we need to go somewhere to avoid getting bored. It's still a couple of weeks before our next guests, my Mum and little sister Emily, so we pluck up courage to cross over to Martinique. Amazingly after more than six months on board El Oro, this is the first sail we've ever done with just the two of us. The litany of things that have gone wrong in the past hangs over us and we set off nervously.

We start badly. The anchor comes up slowly with the chain jamming in the hawser. Once we eventually get that sorted and tidied away, we hoist the mizzen. When it's up we motor sail out of Rodney Bay and without warning lose the port engine. It looks like an electrical issue, and we briefly consider turning back and re-anchoring to sort it out. We push on, but accidentally crash gybe the mizzen. The wind whips the boom across with a huge bang and we look back convinced we've caused some irreparable damage.

Fortunately, there's no harm done, and we safely gybe back and get onto our course. I put the autohelm on, whip off the wheel and take the cover off the control panel. Sure enough, there's a loose electrical connection below it which I'm able to fix and we get Penelope going once more. RL earlier nicknamed the two engines Penelope (port) and Stacey (starboard) and this stuck. From there we get more settled and motor sail comfortably under mizzen and stay sail across to St Annes.

It's less crowded in St Annes than the previous time we were there, however there are still lots of boats anchored off the beach. It's blowing hard when we come in to anchor and we drag some distance before eventually holding with plenty of chain out. The bottom is a mix of sand, rock and broken coral and we drag the anchor into a large clump of rocks where it wedges firm. It shouldn't go any further, but I'm worried about whether we'll be able to get it up again.

The wind continues to blow hard for the next couple of days and we don't feel very secure off St Anne's, so we move round the corner to our familiar haunt in Le Marin. Fortunately, the anchor comes out of its bed of rocks without a hitch, and we weave our way through the various reefs that surround the entrance to this port. As we come around the bend, we avoid a large red ship moored in the channel with a crane lifting yachts aboard. It's getting towards the end of the season, and this is one way to get your boat back to Europe.

We're sitting in the laundrette watching our washing flopping around the large tumble dryer when two vaguely familiar faces come in. They're Roberta and Duca who have a YouTube channel called Odd Life Crafting. I've watched some of their videos and feel like I know them. They are chatty and easy going and we end up inviting them over to El Oro for a drink. They don't drink, they tell us but would love to come over. They end up coming aboard for a coffee a couple of days later and bring another young couple with them. A young Canadian girl called Taylor and her giant of a boyfriend, Kiki. Taylor is also a YouTuber and has a channel called Taylor's Travels. This features her in boats, camper vans or on bikes usually wearing a bikini. She has her life much more together than most 20 somethings that we know and what she has achieved is impressive; sailing across from the US, running her own business and building significant numbers of YouTube subscribers. She and Kiki are also great fun, and we enjoy their company.

Both couples are selling their boats – in fact Ro and Duca

have already sold theirs and are in negotiations to build a larger aluminium boat in France. It's so interesting getting an insight into how their on-line life and business works. They negotiate cash and 'in kind' support in return for product placement as well as maximising views on their channel and they are very savvy at making this work for them.

Once they're gone, Til and I spend a few more quiet nights in our sheltered anchorage in Le Marin before making our way back to Rodney Bay, anchoring offshore from the St Lucia Yacht Club. We have the last couple of days to ourselves before my Mum and youngest sister Emily arrive on Sunday 16 April.

The question of where to go after leaving the Caribbean is one that's been on our minds for a while. The hurricane season officially starts 1 June, and we want to be far away long before then. Some boats go south to Trinidad or other South American destinations for the off-season, the thinking being anywhere south of the 10th parallel is out of the danger zone. Alternatively, we could take the boat north, back to where we started. We know from experience the New England coast would be pleasant to cruise during summer. Tim, however, suggests we bring El Oro across to the Mediterranean. Kent is based there, so longer term it would be easier for him to manage both boats. This is an intriguing idea as it involves crossing the Atlantic, something I've always wanted to do. It's also a big undertaking, at least 3,500 miles of ocean and will require a lot of planning to pull off. Where we'll go once in the Mediterranean is another question. It's a big place. There is a vague discussion over email about leaving El Oro in Tunisia for a refit, but that plan evolves several times. Eventually we agree we'll make for the Greek Islands before handing the boat back. Later Tim calls again to ask how I feel about doing the Atlantic crossing. 'Committed to making it happen,' I say, although in truth it's not without some trepidation. The litany of problems we've had on the boat weigh on my mind. The yacht transporter moored in the mouth of the channel to Le Marin might be an attractive option.

Since then, we've been in contact with family and friends, on a recruitment drive, sounding them out to see if they could join the crossing. Several are interested, but very few can take the time to do the whole journey, so it looks like we'll need to break it into several legs. Til also decides coming down the Atlantic was enough of a long passage for her and she's ready for a break on land. She will get off the boat when we leave the Caribbean and re-join in Portugal.

We're contacted by Les Crane who is organising the Antigua Bermuda race. El Oro has done this race before and Les wants to know if we're up for this year's event, the first running of the race since the end of the pandemic. Bermuda is 900 miles north of Antigua, relatively close to the US coast, and to the casual observer doesn't appear to be on the route to Europe. The circular nature of the weather systems, however, make it necessary to head north before going east to avoid a big area of high pressure in the middle of the Atlantic known as the Azores high. Antigua to Bermuda should be about a week's sail, so could be the perfect first leg of the crossing. With Tim and Kent's encouragement we sign up. I'm not particularly competitive about the race, but there is some security in having the race organisation track our progress. Now all we need is some crew to join us.

Mum and Emily arrive in Rodney Bay after the usual long taxi ride from the St Lucia airport. They've come to help get the boat as far as Antigua. We don't allow them much time to settle in, beginning our journey first thing the next morning. We fill up with fuel and water before heading out of the bay. The crossing is calm compared with earlier passages, but when the yacht heels to the breeze as we round Fort Rodney there's a gasp and a whimper from Emily. She has a nervous disposition and is prone to panic attacks. She grips the cockpit rail in terror, and we encourage her to go below and lie down for a while. Later she emerges briefly but is petrified by the movement of the boat. There's not much we can do at this stage, but things improve when we get into the lee of Martinique, and she recovers.

We make good time and it's smooth sailing as we reach along the west coast of the island up to Saint Pierre. As we near the anchorage with engines on, the revs on Stacey, our starboard engine, dip a couple of times before it splutters and dies. I get out the bleed spanners and Til turns over the engine to try and push the fuel through. A couple of attempts later the engine won't turn over. The battery is flat.

We can try and work this out when we stop for the evening, so we push on. Near the anchorage, Penelope flashes up a red warning light on the dashboard and it looks like we're going to lose her too. We quickly plan around double engine failure, looking at some possible anchorages downwind we can sail back to but it's not necessary as we limp in and drop the hook safely.

Once securely anchored we have a look at the engine batteries more closely and I'm alarmed to discover that aside from the flat one, the other battery is also low as is the smaller battery for the generator; we'll need to keep a close eye on these. We hook up some jumper leads from our working engine and Til once again cranks the motor. I crack the nuts on the injectors and a moment later I can see fuel being pushed through and I close off the nuts and the engine bursts into life. It's a sweet sound.

Saint Pierre is a sleepy settlement and very little is happening when we take the dinghy ashore the next morning. There's a small fruit and vegetable market where we spend the last of our euros. Along the main street there are some old buildings that survived the devastating volcano that wiped out the city in 1902 and there's an impressive cathedral in the process of being restored. We don't linger and an hour or so later are on our way towards Dominica. The crossing is uneventful apart from the occasional stifled gasp from poor Emily who is regretting coming on a sailing holiday. We have a good breeze on the quarter up the coast of Dominica allowing us to avoid the difficult anchorage at Roseau and sail most of the way to Prince Rupert's Bay. Once there we're greeted by Elvis in his battered purple and yellow runabout who looks a little disappointed when we tell him we're in transit and won't be going ashore.

Next morning, we almost sink the boat. We hoist the mizzen and are heading out of the bay when a loud alarm sounds. It takes a few moments to locate the source of the noise as it's not an alarm we've heard before. It's a continuous high-pitched wail we eventually trace to a plastic cover under one of the seats in the saloon. Ominously, it's labelled 'High Water Bilge Alarm'. We quickly pull up the floorboards, but the saloon is dry. We look forward between the two heads and that's also dry. Same thing in our stern cabin. The alarm is loud and driving us crazy so I pull the wire out of the connection to stop it, later realising there's a switch that would do the same thing more easily. Once the alarm stops, we hear water running; it's coming from the engine room.

We open the door, and the water is up over the raised floor. There's seawater gushing in through the stern gland as if from a high-pressure hose. We flick on the bilge pumps, but the water continues to rise. It's coming in faster than the pumps can get rid of it. Til gets a bucket and organises a bailing conga line with my Mum and Emily who paradoxically is calmer now there is something genuinely to panic about. For a little while we achieve an equilibrium, the pumps and bucket action matching the influx of water. As this is going on, I make a call to Kent who thankfully picks up and we talk through the situation. He suggests the problem is either structural, in which case we're in trouble, or it's a failure in the dripless seal which should be more manageable. He explains to me how the dripless seals on the shafts are supposed to work and what I should be looking for. He also recommends I have a look at some online videos on YouTube – not something I have time for at this point.

While this is going on we take a few moments to hastily drop the sails and head back into towards land. If we're going to sink, I'd prefer to be within swimming distance of the shore. Til, Mum and Emily continue to work in a relay bucketing water out of the engine room. Unfortunately, they're losing the battle. The big bilge pump overheats and stops working and the water is now coming in faster than they can get rid of it. It inches back up over the floorboards, lapping around the engine mounts. The heat in the engine room is fierce, we've had the generator on that morning as well as both main engines. After a few minutes in the enclosed space, we're dripping with sweat. There's not much talking, just a quiet determination to save the boat.

Leaning over the back of the engine, torch in one hand, I grab the rubber seal. It's concertina shaped and I pull it forward until it meets the stainless-steel disc screwed to the propeller shaft. Instantly, the water flow slows to a few drips. Unfortunately, the spring in the concertina seal means it won't stay in this position and every time I let go, it slips back and water gushes in once again. I run to the front of the boat and scrabbling under one of the forward berths, pull out the handsaw and an offcut of wood and cut a couple of wedges. After some trial and error, I get these jammed behind the rubber seal, pushing it forward. This slows the ingress buying us some breathing space to get the water to a more manageable level. Thankfully, the phone coverage off that part of Dominica is good and I get Kent on a video call inside the engine room. He suggests the stainless-steel disc may have slipped forward along the shaft, so it no longer abuts the graphite pad on the end of the rubber seal. Now the water is no longer flooding in, I can take some time to have a closer look. Using an allen key and trying to avoid being burned by the hot engine, I loosen the various grub screws securing the rotor disc to the shaft and push it back tight against the rubber seal, compressing the latter by a few centimetres. I tighten up the screws and re-attach the clamp and the boat is once again sealed.

It takes a while to settle before we can set sail again as we're all in shock. The speed we transitioned from a normal departure, to almost losing the boat, was astounding and terrifying. We're distrustful of the seals now and nervous of using the engine. The seal doesn't look right compared with its counterpart on the other engine; the concertina seems too bunched up. It's working however, and no water is coming in. In the afternoon we galvanise ourselves and make the short crossing to the Saints where we anchor in Anse Galet which turns out to be a windy and exposed channel. Our anchor holds firm however and we sleep fitfully, exhausted after the drama of the day.

We had planned to have a rest day in the Saintes, but the weather is windy, and the anchorage is not conducive to lingering so after a morning swim dodging sargasso weed we pull up the anchor and head north once more. We start well with the wind abaft the beam and flat seas across the straits to Guadeloupe. We check the seals on the prop shaft every few minutes, half expecting to see water gushing in. I'm not sure if it's imagination, but it seems as if the starboard shaft is vibrating more than the port one. It has always vibrated, ever since we were in the US, and we'd previously concluded it must be slightly out of alignment, however it seems more pronounced now. We pin it to minimise the risk of further trouble.

Once pinned, we go to start Penelope, our other engine but it's dead. There's nothing showing on the gauge when I turn the key. We're cruising under autopilot, so I whip the wheel off and fiddle with the wiring under the dash. There's a loose connection and the ignition lights come on when the wires are waggled, but they won't stay on. After more fiddling and the use of one of Til's paintbrushes as a wedge, we get the problem temporarily fixed and we motor sail up the coast to another windy and exposed anchorage at Deshaies.

Deshaies is marked on the chart as a deep indentation near the north of the island. It turns out to be a windswept bight with a sleepy village tucked behind. The anchorage is crowded, and we end up dropping the hook in deep water out of the back of the other boats. Bullets of wind scud across the bay and the snubber strains as we surge back and forth in the choppy water. Getting into town means getting soaked as we motor the dinghy directly into the breeze. Coming back is much quicker and easier.

In the morning we have some trouble raising the anchor. We've laid 70M of chain, so it takes a long time to raise it. First the chain keeps jumping off the gypsy – it seems the back half of the chain is a larger diameter to the front which is a bit strange. Next the windlass gets stuck on. The only way we can stop it is to press the down button causing the breaker to trip, stopping it dead. This happens repeatedly but eventually we get all the chain up. Later, we work out the solenoid has stuck, and the pin is locked in the 'on' position. A gentle tap with a hammer solves the problem for now.

It's a long crossing as the breeze softens as we head north. Gradually Antigua appears as a grey smudge under some high clouds, becoming a more defined skyline as we close the coast. It takes us a bit over seven hours to cover the forty miles from Guadeloupe and it is late afternoon before we drop anchor in the shelter of Falmouth Harbour. The contrast with Deshaies is remarkable. It's calm and still and El Oro sits like an obedient labrador, held in check by the weight of her anchor chain.

We spend the next little while recuperating and doing some light maintenance. Til takes Em sunbaking on Pigeon beach. Now we've made it to Antigua she's finally enjoying the trip. Mum and Em leave us a couple of days later, and we are on our own once again. It's Antigua Classic week and immaculately varnished masterpieces are everywhere. They move on after the week finishes to be replaced by a fleet of more conventional racing craft for Antigua Sailing week.

We meet up with a couple, Jamie and Lucy Telfer who have been sailing around the world for the last 10 years. They have circumnavigated the globe via the Cape of Good Hope and now are settled in the Caribbean. They're onto their third boat and are now sailing an Amel 54, a comfortable and seaworthy cruising ketch. They don't own a house – and are committed to their peripatetic lifestyle. They tell us about some hikes out to the high ground above English Harbour and we try out a couple over the next few days. The first one is easy enough but the second nearly causes Til and I to have coronaries. Although we get going early, the day quickly heats up and the route takes us up and over a series of steep arid hills. We're unfit after months on the boat and the sweat streams from us. At the high point, we look out through stinging eyes across the sparkling blue water to Monserrat and Guadeloupe whilst surrounded by crumbling ruins from Nelson's time. It's worth the effort.

MAY

We work through the list of chores knocking off a couple a day as we get the boat ready to head across the ocean to Europe. I service the engines changing the oil and all the filters. I take apart the windlass solenoid and spend a day cursing as I struggle to put it back together again. The wire connections break when taking` the case apart and despite my best soldering efforts refuse to stick back together. Eventually in frustration I drill through the lid of the plastic box and connect the wires directly before filling the holes with sticky white Sikaflex. Hopefully it remains watertight.

The routine comes to an end when the crew arrives for the first leg of the Atlantic crossing. My middle sister Leafy is the first to arrive, followed shortly by Eckhart. The outboard is playing up, so we have a stop start trip to the dinghy dock to pick them up. It's good to have some new people on board, we're ready for company. Eck is Australian but grew up in Namibia and is a friend of a friend, Philip, who will also be joining in a couple of days. I have met him once before, sailing on Philip's J24. Instantly he makes himself useful on board and is soon ensconced in the engine room. Leafy has bought some new set screws for the dripless shaft seal and I want to adjust the way the seal is seated. When we had the drama in Dominica, I had to shove the seal together quickly to stop the flow of water and I'm keen to tackle it again more slowly to ensure it's seated in the right place. We adjust the seal with very little water flowing in and Eck diagnoses the original problem stemmed from a missing hose clamp. We replace this and I'm now much happier about the set up.

The afternoon after they arrive, we pull the anchor up and head east to Nonsuch Bay to give the newcomers some practice with the boat. Unfortunately, it's me that needs the practice, and we get the main halyard caught around the lower runner as we try and hoist the sail. This has the effect of breaking the top car holding the main in the mast track, although we don't notice this until we stow the sail later in the day.

We have a good beat up the coast in a fresh breeze and learn some useful lessons tacking and switching over the runners. We've hardly tacked the boat in the past 8 months, so it's good to have a refresher before the race. We anchor at the back of Green Island in an idyllic spot behind the reef and enjoy a sheltered night. The island is covered with large succulents that look like agave plants. They are flowering and their gigantic stems turn the barren landscape into a surreal forest.

Breaking the car on the main is annoying right before our trip and we leave Nonsuch early in the morning to get to the sailmakers in Falmouth before they shut at Saturday lunchtime.

It turns out we needn't have bothered to rush as our search for a replacement is fruitless. Neither of the two sailmakers have anything that fits, and we have no luck at the chandlery either. We end up sewing a fixed plastic slug as a replacement – something we later find out doesn't work.

Next day the remaining crew arrive; my cousin Michael and his girlfriend Eleanor come together with Philip and later that evening we're joined by an Irish Australian friend, William who comes empty handed as the airline has lost his baggage. None of the crew has done an ocean crossing before and several have never done an overnight passage. It'll be a steep learning curve for all of us.

Our final day passes in a blur of last-minute activity. We take El Oro into the Antigua Yacht Club Marina to fill up with water and end up deciding to stay there. Docking is less than graceful as we are blown off by a strong easterly breeze and it takes a lot of heaving to get the boat gradually into the dock. The dock itself has no cleats which doesn't make it easier. It is designed for enormous super yachts and boats must tie up onto gigantic chains strung along the face of the pontoons. This involves lying prostrate on the wharf and passing the mooring line through the chain and back to the boat. It's not easy to do when it's windy and the boat is being blown the other way.

We're moored next to a vast black and chrome superyacht called the Alfa Nero. There are two bored security guards stationed on the wharf under a sunshade and a sign indicating it's the property of the Antigua and Barbuda government. The guards tell us the boat belonged to a Russian oligarch but was seized following Russia's invasion of Ukraine. Michael asks the guards if they're worried about the Russians coming back to claim their boat. 'Why? What have you heard?' they ask, looking around uncomfortably. Much later we hear the boat is sold at auction for $67M, about half of the estimated valuation.

We go through immigration formalities to check out of Antigua and check-in to the race. Philip generously organises for a diver to clean the hull and we complete a rash of last-minute tasks before meeting our fellow competitors at the evening drinks party to mark the race. There are six entrants in a range of very different vessels. Nemo is a superfast multihull, it won't take long to get to Bermuda, and there's also a slick looking 60ft racing yacht called Black Pearl. There are a couple of Canadian yachts, Life of Reilly and Bella J, the latter a J133. Both are heading to Halifax in Nova Scotia. There's an X55 called Rye and us. I'm not sure how the handicap system accounts for these wildly different hull types but we're all on the start line the next morning.

It's blowing a stiff north-easterly breeze as we wave goodbye to Til and motor out of the marina before going to hoist the sails. Holding the boat head to wind while the team painstakingly inch the main up the mast track, we are flanked by two of our competitors doing the same thing. We've almost hauled the heavy sail up to the masthead when we see the top slug pull out of the track. It's the temporary plastic one we sewed on a couple of days before and it means we can't get the top of the sail snug against the mast.

We haul the sail down again and quickly ascertain there's nothing we can do to fix the problem. Kent's words are ringing in my ears: if we're racing, I'm responsible for the sails and the rig. Will the missing slug damage the sail? The top of the main won't sit snug against the mast – particularly when there's a reef in the sail. We're about to embark on a 1000-mile offshore race and before we've even started, we've increased the risk of expensive damage.

We battle to get the main back up once again, motoring hard to try and reach the line. We're nearly there and one engine dies on us – a repeat of our earlier ignition issues. As well as the reefed main, we don't deploy the genoa at the start. Tacking the big sail is complicated as we need to go forward and furl it before we go about, so we leave it until we're well under way. This leaves us underpowered, and we wallow in the messy swell. We miss the initial starting signal on the radio and suddenly we hear 'clear start'; the race has begun. Luckily, we're less than fifty metres from the line but it still takes us several minutes to officially begin the race. By the time we cross the line three of our complement are vomiting over the side. I yell in alarm at Michael who is sitting on the windward rail preparing to heave the contents of his stomach – likely to coat all of us in vomit. Eleanor is also being sick, and William has turned a shade of green. We later discover his affliction is more to with the bottle of rum he accounted for the previous night.

The fleet are disappearing over the horizon as we gradually get the boat moving. We unfurl the huge grey headsail and accelerate towards Green Island at the eastern tip of Antigua. Round the corner we ease sheets and hoist the mizzen and soon we're doing over eight knots. After our poor start, we gradually get into the rhythm of the trip; three hours on, six hours off. The first few days are something akin to purgatory, taking forever but time seems to accelerate as we pass the halfway point. The good breeze lasts for the first 48 hours, pushing us 350 miles along our path. At this point we reach the northern limit of the trades, and the wind drops and soon afterwards dies altogether. We try and coax some forward motion out of the boat but after half an hour of the sails banging and slatting in the swell we give up and turn on the engines. Under the rules of the race, competitors are allowed to motor so long as the hours are logged. Bella J ahead of us tries to hold out not motoring and we close the gap until we're level with her. We call her on the VHF, and she fires her engine. The race has become a powerboat competition.

We end up motoring through calm waters for almost 36 hours before the wind returns. It's a chance for the seasick to recover and we dry out the boat. Eventually a light breeze springs up from ahead and the silence is blissful when we switch off both engines. The final days of the race pass quickly. At one point Eck and I take advantage of the calm conditions to work on the generator. For some reason when we're underway an airlock forms in the raw water-cooling system. Seawater won't flow through the heat exchanger, so the engine overheats and shuts itself off. We investigate every hose looking for possible leaks before deciding we need to take the impeller out again. We remove the water pump and have the parts spread across the floor in the engine room. It's a bit inconclusive and we don't find anything wrong, but when we put it back together it seems to work once more.

On line-honours we are ahead of Bella J and Life of Reilly but they've both pipped us on handicap. The wind swings around to the nose as we approach Bermuda, and it takes us half a day to pass the last few miles to the line. We call up Bermuda Radio as instructed to advise of our finish time, and they profess to know nothing about the race! No matter, we email in our time before heading into St George's through the town cut and anchor off the customs wharf. Remembering the scary customs lady who processed us last time we were in Bermuda, I warn everyone to be on their best behaviour. The crew look at me as if I've lost the plot when we're cleared in and welcomed by the friendliest official I've ever come across. After the paperwork's done, we go to the bar and get a sharp reminder we're in Bermuda. A round of beers at the Whitehorse Pub set us back over $100.

16th May dawns warm and sunny, and in the morning, we motor back out of the cut on our way to Hamilton on the other side of the island. We omit to call up Bermuda radio to obtain clearance to go through the cut which elicits a shirty call from them. They have eyes on everyone. Three hours later we come alongside the breakwater at the Royal Bermuda Yacht Club and Les Crane, the race organiser, and Reggie Houseman, the marina manager, help us with our lines. They are extremely welcoming, and we enjoy a pleasant few days at the club. We work through the list of repairs and do some exploring around the island. William shouts us all dinner at the Lobster Shack which must have been hideously expensive and later Michael and Eleanor take us for dinner at Elbow Beach on the south of the island. The weather has changed and it's cold and windy although we still brave a swim in the turquoise waters before shivering on a dilapidated terrace of a run-down resort.

William heads home, still without his bag, and we leave Michael and Eleanor in Hamilton as we head back to St George's to pick up new crew. We've planned to stop next at the Azores, a tiny group of islands far out in the Atlantic 1,800 miles away, before going on to Portugal. Leafy, Eck and Philip are staying on to do the full crossing and we have four new crew joining us in Bermuda.

Rob and his daughter Mia arrive minus a missing bag and a day later Johnnie and Roscoe; the latter also with a missing bag and the former with two hard suitcases which elicits some gentle ribbing and challenges with stowage. Roscoe's bag turns up the day before we depart but Mia and Rob take a bus trip into Hamilton to buy new wet weather gear as there is no sign of their stuff.

We're anchored in Powder Hole, across the bay from the town when the heavens open. A deep low has moved up from the Caribbean and it rains torrentially for the final days of our stay in Bermuda. The boat is a dripping steam box as we keep everything closed to avoid too much water getting below. We pour over the weather forecast comparing the different models;

we'll either go Wednesday evening or Thursday morning. The biblical rain continues to lash down and is accompanied by strong gusting southerly winds. Wednesday morning has a brief lull, and we take the opportunity to head across to the fuel dock. This is the same dock we struggled to get off all those months previously with Kent and I'm keen to get in while the wind is quiet. Unfortunately, as we motor across from our anchorage, another squall scuds through and visibility reduces to nothing as we are hit again by driving rain and wind. We motor slowly in circles getting drenched until it passes when we make our way in, handing up some very sodden lines to the waiting fuel attendants.

At five pm it's still windy but the rain has stopped; it's time to get going. It's not a quick process – we clear customs who need to see in person all the guys who have flown in over the past few days. Some of these have taken the opportunity to go last-minute shopping so we round them up and eventually get the paperwork done.

It's reassuring having more experienced crew on board for this leg. Philip, Leafy and Eck now have a good feel for the boat, and they also know where everything is stowed; not an easy thing to work out on El Oro. Of the new team, Rob is an airline pilot and has worked for Qantas for 30 years. He has a calming presence and is good in a crisis. I've done plenty of offshore sailing with him including the Sydney Hobart race a couple of times on Mille Sabords, his Sydney 38. His daughter Mia is less experienced, but she's enthusiastic and brave and it's good to have some youth on board. Roscoe is good mates with Rob, and he also sailed with us on Mille Sabords. Johnnie is an old friend who I've known since first moving to Australia 30 years ago. We've been on a charter holiday years ago, but he's not done a huge amount of sailing.

Leaving in the evening allows us to take advantage of fresh

favourable winds and get a head start of 100 miles by dawn. It is also a difficult way for the new crew to adjust to the boat and Mia and Roscoe are seasick as we corkscrew through the strong chop. Rain and squalls persist throughout the night adding to the misery for the newbies. At one stage we find ourselves in a violent thunderstorm with lightening flashing around us and accompanying peals of thunder alarmingly close. Johnnie is OK but it's been a long while since he's spent any time on a yacht, and he takes a while to get his sea legs. We leave Bermuda in company with Seabird, a 70ft Oyster with five people on board, also heading to the Azores. For the first few days we keep in contact over the VHF. They give us an HF frequency to contact them, but none of us can master the HF set we have on board and we're unable to raise them or hear them once we fall out of VHF range.

We're not on our own however, as there's a surprising amount of shipping. Each day we see several AIS plots showing ships coming to and fro either from the US coast or from Europe. Occasionally they come close enough to see, but we're glad we have the AIS to help us keep a look out.

After a couple of days, we break free from the band of rain that has been dogging us since Bermuda and we enjoy some calmer weather. Up goes the red stripey mizzen staysail and we lollop along gently imagining the remainder of our trip in shorts and T shirts. Johnnie experiments with the fishing gear and we almost have some success with the plain wooden lure our neighbour at the Royal Bermuda Yacht Club gave us. He puts it out at dawn and shortly after there's a huge strike and afterwards there's no lure on the end of our line. We can only imagine the monster that has made off with the tackle. Unfortunately, this is the nearest we'll get to catching a fish on this leg.

We download the various weather models over the Iridium

Go. The weather ahead is unsettled, and the models show different forecasts. Before we lost them, Seabird told us they were using the services of a professional weather router from the States, and we're keen to get their view on which way to go. They tell us they're going south to avoid a developing low-pressure system. Conventional orthodoxy suggests heading north to the 40th parallel before turning east to get on top of the Azores high. This year however there isn't a formed high, instead a series of lows that seem to form from nowhere and roll through.

Gradually it becomes apparent there will be some heavy weather ahead and we decide to take Seabird's approach and make sure we get on the south side of the depression which should keep the wind behind us. Unfortunately, by now we're out of contact with Seabird so can't get an update from their router. We prepare the boat as best we can, making sure everything is well stowed as well as getting out the storm jib and putting a second reefing line in the mizzen. While doing this we are interrupted by an occasional sharp beep; it could be low battery on the smoke alarm. We remove the battery, and the alarm continues, beeping once every 30 seconds or so. Perhaps because I'm tired after a few days getting into our watch routine it takes me a while to comprehend this is the high-water bilge alarm being triggered by water sloshing in the bilge.

We pull up some floorboards and sure enough there is a large volume of water surging to and fro. My first thought is we have a leaking through-hull fitting once again. We're around 600 miles offshore, so not a great place to be taking on water. We methodically check every seacock, and the propeller shaft seals, and nothing seems wrong. The electric bilge pumps are weak and struggle to remove the volume of water. This is something we need to address when we get to the Azores and something I should have fixed in Bermuda. Right now, we turn to the hand bilge pump in the cockpit, pulling water out into a bucket which we tip overboard. This works better and we remove multiple buckets of dirty brown water.

Once we get the water out and it's clear no more is flooding in, we can think more clearly about where it could have come from. We consider the freshwater tanks which seem emptier than they should be. Potentially they are leaking? Later we discard this theory as the volume seems to be remaining constant. It's more likely the water is rainwater from the huge deluge we had in Bermuda and our first night or two at sea. On investigation there's a crack in the cockpit drain funnelling water into the engine room rather than straight out to sea. There's also water coming in through the anchor hawser pipe and running the length of the bilge.

Gradually the weather models converge with a large depression forming somewhere around Bermuda and passing over to the north of us. Before it gets to us, we are hit by strong headwinds, and we gradually reduce sail. The large genoa is the first to come in followed by a reef in the mizzen to temper the weather helm. The wind continues to rise and although the seas aren't huge, we're bashing into a short ugly chop bringing green water over the deck with every wave. Despite having the dorade covers on, much of this finds its way through hatches and vents and bedding and clothing in the forward cabins is soon soaked.

The boat is heeled over at 40 degrees, and we can see blue water streaming past the leeward portholes. We leave taking the main down a little longer than we should and we're tearing along. The boat judders as we fly off the back of a wave and slam into the trough below. I look across at Nelson's decanter on the other side of the saloon. It's secured with a wooden holder screwed into the hull so it's not going anywhere, but from the corner of my eye I spot the stopper bouncing in the crystal neck. It's time to reduce sail and we set to the task. The wind is now blowing a full gale and we have all hands on deck trying to subdue the heavy mainsail. It jams in the track, and we struggle to haul down the wet flogging fabric. Horizontal rain makes it impossible to look forward and we battle on through half closed eyes. Five people are lined up along the boom trying to gather in the sail and it takes all their strength and co-ordination to get it securely lashed with sail ties.

Eventually we get it packed away and we're more in control. We take a second reef in the mizzen so now are as snug as we can be in the gale. It's frustrating not having a wind speed indicator but the forecast is telling us it should be thirty knots which must be gusting well over forty. Gradually the wind veers as the low moves over us and the wind angle comes further aft. The boat flattens out and we are more comfortable. Periodically I check the bilge and there's some water coming in – but nothing too alarming. Most of this is likely flowing through the boat from the anchor chain hawser which we tried unsuccessfully to block with a rag.

The wind continues strong for the next 48 hours. The low is moving slowly and in the same direction as us, so it doesn't pass through quickly. Later in the day, we hear some radio chatter about a yacht called Le Chercheur issuing a Mayday. It seems the French authorities have picked up an EPIRB signal and passed it to the US coastguard for attention. They in turn have contacted nearby ships and it's these that we've heard.

Amazingly, Le Chercheur shows up on our AIS a few moments later; it's about 5 miles ahead of us. We call them on the VHF, and I get onto a Frenchman with limited English. He is very stressed, telling us they are taking on water. They've issued a Mayday and are abandoning ship. There's a tanker coming to their rescue. We ask them if they'd like us to standby until the ship arrives and they say no – the sea state is too bad, and we should go on.

Shortly after we receive a call from the ship that is approaching them – the Overseas Santorini. We let him know what we've seen, and the captain asks us to stay by the yacht until he gets there as he won't be there until after dark. We heave to and shadow the distressed yacht, a Beneteau Oceanis 32. It's a very small and lightly built boat to be out in the middle of the ocean in bad weather. We have some further conversations on the radio, and they tell us they have two children on board aged five and eight – a fact we relay to the approaching ship. The couple on board sound increasingly distressed and there are shouts in the background about l'eau.

There is a language barrier between the Captain of the Santorini who's American and the French yacht, and the captain asks if we have any French speakers on board. We tell him we'll try our best – although none of us has anything beyond school level French. The captain issues instructions about how the ship will approach, and what he wants the yacht to do, which we do our best to relay in terrible Franglais. 'Le grand bateau va approcher,' I say to Le Chercheur over the radio, before looking to the El Oro crew bunched together in the cockpit. 'Is that a reflexive verb?' I ask. There's a sea of blank looks, so I continue. 'Err... s'approcher, from le starboard side.' The lights of the tanker pierce the gathering gloom as it appears over the horizon and zigzags to take off speed. The tanker captain brings his vessel round in a big circle and ends up to windward of the yacht. He passes some complicated instructions to us about cargo netting and firing lines to the yacht which we struggle to translate. 'What's the word for rope?' We look at each other trying to drag up distant memories of French classes, but there's not much there. 'Ligne? Corde?' We're not sure and try both options. The French family are worried they're going to be asked to get into the water, but we reassure them they should motor up to the side of the ship and the crew will help them board. The cargo net is beyond our language ability, so we try and explain that in English. It's not clear whether the instructions are understood but the yacht moves towards the ship. We can't see the moment of transfer as we're keeping well clear but a couple of minutes later the captain calls us to let us know everyone is safely on board. The yacht is simply abandoned, a small handkerchief of sail still up. We presume it will soon sink.

There's some discussion about whether we should try and get on board and attempt to salvage the vessel. 'That boat's French,' says Philip, 'it's bound to have some good wine and cheese on board'. It's now dark, it's rough and the boat's sinking so I veto the idea and we watch their navigation lights gradually fade behind us into the night.

JUNE

THE LOW-PRESSURE ZONE eases off before reforming into a second depression and the wind and rain stay with us. We steer southeast to keep the wind behind the beam and make fast progress through the lumpy seas with the staysail and reefed mizzen. Working the series of watches, we get into a rhythm. The days blur into each other as we do our three hours on and six hours off. Without reference to the log, it's soon impossible to gauge how long we've been at sea. We gather in the evening around 5.30pm for a drink and try and have dinner together. Philip has taken over from Til as the main chef and works doggedly to produce meals under the most trying conditions. He straps himself into the galley juggling pressure cookers on the small stovetop. He's not the only one using the galley as Johnnie has taken to making a daily loaf of bread.

There's a bread maker built into the cooktop, and he pulls the ingredients together during the night watch, so we wake to the smell of freshly baked bread. Eck experiments with the bread maker to bake a tea cake which works surprisingly well so this also becomes a regular feature on the menu. There's nearly an awkward moment when Johnnie accidently uses Eck's special cake flour for one of his loaves of bread, but good humour prevails.

Eventually, 24 hours out from the Azores, the weather relents, and the sun comes out. We see a couple of whales and a pod of dolphins, almost the only sea life we've seen on this leg. We're making for Flores, the outermost island of the archipelago. According to the pilot book most yachts skip this and head direct for Horta on Faial but I'm keen to visit the most westerly point in Europe.

It's 3.00am when we get there. We could wait until daylight to get in but there's a full moon and visibility is good. The interior of the island is high and the ridgeline very dark against the night sky. We creep slowly past the cliffs at the south of the island and round the flashing red marker into Porto das Lajes. We come inside a concrete breakwater, smashed to bite size bits by a hurricane a few years earlier. The harbour is narrow and on the other side there's a wharf with a brightly lit coaster being loaded with goods which must be the supply ship for the island. We drop our anchor in the middle of the small harbour and turn the engines off after sailing almost 2,000 miles from Bermuda.

It's a steep walk to the top of the hill above the harbour. Strongly built houses cling to the hillside surrounded by lush green grass and black rock. We pop our head into the police station and ask about immigration. 'Don't worry,' we're told. 'They'll find you.' We find a café and enjoy a coffee overlooking the Atlantic. It's a relief to look at the ocean without being on it.

We stay a couple of days in port but there's a new approaching weather system which looks dangerous. There's a small inner harbour at Lajes for the fishing fleet; this might be safe but we're much too big to get into it. The new system will bring strong winds from the east so our anchorage will be very exposed. I call the marina at Horta, 120 miles to the east but they tell us they have no room, and we should head for shelter at Punta Delgada. We consult the chart; that's nearly 300 miles away and there's no way we'll get there before the storm hits. We need to seek shelter elsewhere on Flores.

There are no other defined harbours marked on the chart, but we can see there are some indentations on the west coast which could give shelter in an easterly. The wind is building and it's wet and sploshy getting out in the dinghy from the wharf in Lajes. To make matters worse we have a repeat of the outboard problems that plagued us in Antigua. The motor is difficult to start and keeps cutting out. Once running, it pours fuel from the carburettor. Eck and I take the time before leaving to again strip it down and clean it out. We're convinced we've taken on a load of dirty fuel in Antigua and sure enough find globs of muck gumming up the nozzles.

Once round the southern tip of the island we motor slowly up the west coast. It's wonderfully remote; usually this is the windward side battered by Atlantic storms and it's rarely visited. There are high black volcanic cliffs fringed with lush vegetation. White foaming streams of water rush down the hillside and tumble into the sea. Near the water's edge pillars of rock protrude from the black water and guard the approach to shore.

We anchor in a deep sheltered bay bordered by steep cliffs and dark jagged rocks. There's no one else here, the only sign of life is a goat marooned halfway down the cliff with no apparent way to get off. It's not clear if the goat is stuck there or is there by choice, but it seems content. We swim, shower in the waterfall and Johnnie even catches a fish. It's a trigger fish and the book on board says these are a risk of carrying ciguatera poisoning if they're over 5kg. We have a big debate over the weight of the fish but in the end, we cook it anyway and it's delicious. We are slightly put out when another boat joins us late in the evening; a French couple who have also made their way across the Atlantic.

We sit out the gale in perfect comfort before heading off for Faial the following evening. Although the storm has passed, we have 20kts of wind hard on the nose and it's an uncomfortable and slow crossing. Eventually in the afternoon we make out the high ground of Faial and behind it, the even higher shape of Pico. This is a perfect picture book volcano over 7,000 ft high.

We don't get to Horta until late afternoon and make our way through the gap in the breakwater to find the anchorage extremely crowded. We take several attempts to anchor before settling ourselves in a narrow gap between two liveaboards. It's a rough dinghy ride ashore against the wind to clear customs and check in but well worth the ride as Jose in the marina offers us a berth against the fuel wharf for the princely sum of 45EUR. At that price it's tempting to stay for a month, but we end up staying three very sociable days. Every yacht looking to fill up with fuel must raft up next to us and we have a good yarn with all of them. Several are young families looking to make their way back to Europe after spending time adventuring in the Caribbean. Others are seasoned travellers who have been at sea for years and are very familiar with this nautical crossroads.

We spend a lazy few days recuperating after our crossing. We explore the town and enjoy the music festival taking place each evening in the park. There's some weird act with mermaids that makes no sense, but it's a good spectacle. There's lots of discussion about taking a ferry across to Pico and climbing the volcano but somehow, we never get around to it. We do some reprovisioning and Leafy paints a likeness of El Oro on the wall beside the marina. This is a tradition and there are hundreds, or perhaps thousands of yacht names and images painted around the dock area. We can't see any dating before the 1990s so presumably people paint over old images when they can't find new space. We find an out of the way spot on a wall above an electricity substation where our image should last longer.

Reluctantly we need to move on if we're going to get to Punta Delgada in time to pick up our next crewmembers and we disentangle ourselves from the fuel wharf where we have three boats tied up outside us. It's a broad reach along the channel between Pico and Sao Jorges and for the first time we hoist the asymmetric spinnaker, gliding across the flat water at ten knots. When we reach the end of Sao Jorges, we drop the kite and harden up onto the wind to cross over the 20 miles or so to Terceira arriving late in the evening. It's Portugal day and the crew are keen to get ashore to enjoy the festivities. We can hear the boom of a cannon and loud partying from the shoreline. The dinghy is craned into the water, and everyone piles in but sits in disappointment as Eck pulls the starter cord again and again with no hint of ignition. After ten minutes of frustration, they give up and climb back on board and the dinghy is hoisted back onto the davits again.

It's 80 miles to Sao Miguel and we leave early, the high ground behind us fading into the haze, as we motor east in windless conditions. The chart is black with contour lines, there's a mysterious seamount on our path where the sea floor rises from 2000 metres to six metres deep, but we don't see anything except for an endless expanse of smooth water. The day remains calm, and we chug steadily into mid-afternoon, the blue outline of Sao Miguel gradually materialising on the far horizon. The western end of the island is dominated by the rim of a gigantic volcanic crater. It doesn't take much imagination to see how it would have looked; classically shaped like Pico before a massive eruption blew off the top. We close the coast and follow the southern shoreline until we come to Punta Delgada. A long concrete breakwater runs outside the port with several ships tied up alongside including a magnificent square rigger. It's Sunday evening and everything is closed so we try and come alongside the reception wharf planning to wait there until Monday morning. Unfortunately, there's no room so we push on to the western harbour. The marina is full of boats participating in the AZAB regatta, a race from Falmouth in the UK to the Azores and Back. There are boats of all shapes and sizes including an IMOCA as well as various small cruiser racers. We spy one free berth in an accessible spot on the corner. It's a bit small for us but it's our only option. The wind, which has been non-existent all day now pipes up from the beam and as we glide in, we are pushed sideways into the edge of the berth. Our fenders are too high and there's a horrible crunch as the metal bites into the wooden hull. We secure the boat, at least half our length is sticking out, and settle down for a meal and a drink. We'll address the damage in the morning.

Two hours later it is dark, and we pop up on deck in response to shouts from an angry catamaran owner circling behind us. It seems we're in his berth. He turns round and heads off to the other dock. After a brief discussion we follow him out and catch up to him as he's securing himself to the fuel wharf. We apologise and he becomes more friendly explaining he couldn't get into the berth in any case as he requires both spaces to be free, and there is another smaller boat moored on the other side. We consider rafting up with him at the fuel wharf, but he suggests we go back to his slot in the marina. The crosswind is still blowing so we approach cautiously, nosing back in with no trouble this time around.

In the morning the marina office informs us there is no space whatsoever and unfortunately, we will have to go and sit at anchor. I explain we need to make some repairs to the hull but the official simply shrugs and says he can't help. 'But we are already in a berth – we came in last night.' I say, pointing towards the quay.

'Why didn't you say so? In that case how many nights do you want to stay?'

I start to explain we've stolen someone else's berth, but he waves me away.

'There are no reserved berths on that row – so you can stay there'.

We have a couple of days before Rob and Mia leave us and our new crew, Adam and Perm join so we tackle a list of pending jobs. Top on the list is repairing the damage to the hull we created on the way in. Leafy, who spent a year training as a boatbuilder, comes into her own. She painstakingly sands back all the damaged epoxy and wood beneath before gradually building up new layers of epoxy. She also takes the opportunity to work on some of the other damaged paintwork around the hull. Once she's finished it's almost impossible to see where the repairs have been done.

Rob and Mia leave early the next morning in thick fog and spend most of the day at the airport waiting for their flight to take off. We take the opportunity to hire a car and explore some of the interior. We drive up through the lush green interior along narrow laneways lined with hydrangeas. The hedgerows thick with purple and white flowers. We pass stone walled paddocks and see glimpses of cattle through the wet mist as we climb higher and higher towards the lip of the crater. At the top the mist clears for a few moments and we have a stunning view into the interior where there are two lakes, the Lagoa Azul and the Lagoa Verde. Legend has it a princess fell in love with a common fisherman but wasn't allowed to marry him as he was too low born. Their tears created the two lakes which are close together but don't quite meet.

There's a winding road that leads to the bottom of the crater where the village of Sete Cidades sits on the shore of the Lagoa Azul. Cottages with well-kept vegetable gardens line the small grid of streets. We find a remarkably inexpensive restaurant that produces a delicious lunch and afterwards set off to find a tunnel reputedly built in the 1930s through the wall of the crater. We don't know what we're looking for – whether it's a road tunnel or for pedestrians so it takes us a while but eventually we locate a small brick passageway heading into the hillside. The roof is at head height, and it's pitch dark with water running in an open culvert alongside and sometimes over the rough pathway. We use the torch on our phones to see where we're going, every ten metres marked out on the wall. Ahead there's a tiny pinprick of light and we stumble towards this for 1,250 metres through the mountain until at last we emerge into the sunshine the other side. We're now standing on the road leading to the west coast. 80 years ago, this would have been a quick way out of the village instead of trudging all the way up to the lip of the crater and down the other side.

Perm and Adam join us direct from Melbourne that evening, and we check out the following morning for mainland Portugal. The forecast looks light, and I warn everyone we might be motoring for much of the 900-mile crossing.

It turns out the breeze is light – but there's enough to carry a spinnaker and we end up sailing all the way; the engine doesn't come on until the final hours of the voyage to get us around Cape St Vincent. We hoist the asymmetrical as we know how that works but it's soon clear the wind is too far aft, and we need to deploy the more traditional symmetrical kite. This is sealed deep beneath one of the bunks and we get the screwdriver out to access it. It takes some head scratching to work out how to run all the lines and setup the pole. Our first attempt to hoist almost ends in disaster as we let the kite swing too far forward and it gets caught on the anchor sticking out the front of the boat. There's a sickening tearing sound and we swiftly bring it back on board. Fortunately, the rip is small, so we tape it and try again. This time we get it up without a hitch and the heavy boat almost doubles its speed, accelerating effortlessly from five to nine knots.

Initially we carry this rig through the day, dropping the kite at sunset before setting it once again in the morning. Later when we're more confident we run through the hours of darkness also. The motion is smooth, the boat is under control, and we surge across the flat water. This is champagne sailing at its best.

We quickly and easily fall back into the rhythm of offshore sailing. Watches come and go and the days blend together once again. Happy hour is bought forward by popular request to 4.30pm and there's a cocktail party every evening with music, drinks and snacks before dinner after which we revert to the night-time watch routine. Perm entertains us with stories about his brewery on Magnetic Island, his 34 Sydney to Hobart races and the time he lost one of his toes. We all laugh a lot.

The model on Predict Wind tells us the crossing will take six and half days. I haven't adjusted the polars for the spinnaker however and we consistently beat the model by two to three knots. This means we sight the coast of Portugal, a line of red-brown cliffs stretching low across the horizon, five days after leaving Punta Delgada. The wind finally dies on us as we approach Cape St Vincent, the southwest corner of mainland Europe. The kite comes down and we motor past the imposing lighthouse and on for another twenty miles before entering the river at Portimão.

The marina is on the west bank of the river and is close to the tourist centre of town. In the evening there is a bright strip of neon bars and an endless array of cheap food venues. Loud English voices compete with German, Swedish and other unidentified tongues. A throng of young, sunburned trippers swagger confidently along the street, eyed warily by the tourist police who lean against the wall of the police station twirling their batons. There don't seem to be any local Portuguese around, perhaps we've come to the wrong spot.

It seems we have, but we don't have far to go to get to the more authentic old town. We cross the river the next day looking for a lunch venue and are enticed by a maze of small streets, markets and Portuguese voices. None of last night's crowd seem to have ventured this side of the waterway. We have a long lunch that rolls into evening drinks and dinner. It's the perfect decompression after the crossing and we pile eight people into the dinghy at the end of the night to cross the river unsteadily back to the marina.

In the morning we say goodbye to Leafy and Johnnie. They go early and without fuss, but there's an emptiness without them. It's been such a tight knit crew for each leg and suddenly it's breaking up. In the afternoon we fill up with fuel and leave the marina, moving to the anchorage across the water. Til re-joins us along with Lizzie, Adam's wife, and we have a full complement again, ready to push on towards the Mediterranean.

The entrance to the river at Faro, twenty miles along the coast, is interesting with the flood tide swirling into the estuary and carrying us through at alarming speed. The channel is narrow and twisting and it takes some concentration to keep in the deep water. We nearly have an altercation with a fisherman who is putting out his nets exactly where we want to go but we avoid him ignoring his curses and find a sheltered anchorage in a deep pool near the junction leading up to Olhoa.

It's eighty miles to Cadiz so we're up at the first hint of light. A pink glow illuminates the eastern channel behind us as we backtrack towards the entrance where we came in the previous evening. This time we're at the top of the tide and there's very little current. There are dozens of small fishing boats drifting across the narrow entrance and we have some uncomfortable moments as we weave our way around them.

Later in the morning a stiff breeze springs up and we're close reaching on the port tack. I take a cursory glance into the engine room to check everything is OK and there's a bit of water in the bilge again. It's not full but there's more than there was earlier that morning. This is strange as it hasn't been raining and neither is it particularly rough. Eck comes by with a glass and we take a sample and look at it in the light of day. In the glass there are two liquids, a slightly off coloured one makes up most of the volume and a thin layer of clear liquid underneath. I put my finger in, and it's greasy. It seems we're leaking diesel into the bilge.

This isn't great news, but it does explain a bit. When we filled up in Portimão, I was surprised by how much diesel we'd consumed on the crossing even though we'd hardly run the engines. It's now a question of finding the leak.

There are eight metal diesel tanks on board. We pull up the floorboards and have a look at each in turn. They're all a bit rusty and any one of them looks as if it could be the culprit but we can't see any fuel dripping. The pipes coming in and out of each tank also look dry. I scratch my head wondering what to do next when I recall Kent telling me months before in Rhode Island there is also a spare tank we aren't using. I've never seen this tank but it's somewhere under the galley floor, so we pull up the boards and have a look.

Under the floorboard there's a large fibreglass container painted grey. As soon as we look at it, we know we're on to something. There's fuel sloshing about in the cavity next to it. A moment later the boat heels to a gust of wind and I brace against the sink to stop myself falling over. Beneath me little jets of liquid squirt out all along the seam. The boat comes back on an even keel and the flow of liquid stops. We've found our leak.

The tank is shut off, so it shouldn't fill up when we refuel, however when I look more closely, I notice the diesel return valve is open. Return lines spill out from the engine to each of the tanks like an octopus, returning unused fuel. The valve for the spare tank needs to be shut otherwise the tank is continually topped up whenever the engine's running. The leak is along the seam at the top of the tank on the starboard side so it's only a problem when we're heeling over that way. We tack north to get the boat tilting the other way and turn on the engines. I open the tap on the spare tank and shut off all eight other tanks. After a couple of hours, the starboard engine splutters to a halt and we conclude the tank must be empty. We shut it off before switching back to the main tanks and tack back towards Cadiz.

We're enjoying a peaceful afternoon when the tranquillity is shattered by a series of deep booms. Each report produces a low shockwave that travels right through us. Whilst we were searching for the diesel leak there was some chatter in the background from the VHF. Part of this was a series of 'All Ships' messages from a US warship advising of live firing, and an instruction no one should come within 15 miles of a particular co-ordinate. Because I was head down in the bilge, I vaguely heard the messages but didn't take note of the co-ordinates. We're in a busy shipping lane just outside of the

Mediterranean; surely there can't be much danger here. Perhaps I should have been more careful.

The firing stops and later we spot the warship itself although it makes no contact with us. We push on to the east and in the afternoon the wind becomes stronger directly from where we want to go. We drop the sails and motor again making slow progress over the last few miles through the gulf of Cadiz. The sea is choppy, and the wind keeps building and everything on deck, including us, is soon encrusted in salt spray; a white rime coating every surface. We dodge another warship, a Spanish one this time heading out of the Rota naval base, and eventually we come into the lee of Cadiz anchoring behind the old town at Caleta Beach.

Til and I were last here thirty something years ago, before we were married. I remember it as a romantic city; sandstone buildings with plantation shutters lining small laneways and hidden plazas. It doesn't seem to have changed much in the intervening years. The city sits on the end of a long peninsula and behind the old town is a narrow opening called the Canal del Sur. The opening is lined with fearsome green rocks on both sides that are covered at high tide and there are forts commanding both headlands. At the head of the inlet there's a crowded beach packed with swimmers and sunbathers. To get to the town we beach our dinghy on the sand as there's no wharf and pick our way through the beach towels and brightly coloured umbrellas to the street behind. It's busy and the town is full of tourists and locals alike; walking through the network of small laneways lined with cafes and restaurants is slow going.

I drag everyone off to try and find customs and immigration which turns out to be an unnecessary exercise. We trudge out to the port in the heat of the day, two miles away on the other side of the peninsula, only to be pointed back to the town. Once we locate the relevant authorities, they briefly look at our passports and wave us away. We've come from another European country within the Schengen zone. There's no requirement to check in.

Back at the boat that afternoon we watch a catamaran approach our anchorage. It's coming from the direction of the port and the outcrop of rocks are covered by the high tide. At first, we assume he knows where he's going, he seems so confident. Perhaps there's a gap in the reef the locals know about. If there is, he misses it as there's a crunch and he comes to an abrupt halt. There's some shouting and gesticulating on board and a lot of revving of engines and with a graunch he backs off into deeper water before disappearing sheepishly towards the port.

Adam and Liz leave us to join their daughter Alice who has recently completed a university exchange in the Netherlands. Perm also leaves; he's flying to Ecuador to rendezvous with his latest girlfriend. Philip and Eck head off after nearly two months on board. They've been such an integral part of the boat for so long it's strange without them. Roscoe is the last man standing from the Atlantic crossing; he's committed to accompany us as far as Gibraltar.

I've been so focussed on getting the crew needed for the Atlantic crossing I haven't thought enough about the long Mediterranean passages ahead. Til has done some recruiting while she was in London, but we don't have enough crew. It's 1,500 miles to the Greek Islands and we can't sail El Oro by ourselves. Adam and Liz come to the rescue before they leave, drumming up some support for us. Through their daughter Alice they recruit Tom, a young Australian friend of hers who will join El Oro in Gibraltar. They also convince another friend to join: John, an Australian who's in London sorting out some family issues. He says he'll come straight away and may be able to bring a couple of friends with him.

We also have Ruth and Louisa, friends from Sydney who join us the next day. Neither has done much sailing which is tricky when passage making, but they tell us they're up for the challenge. Ruth will be with us for a few days, but Louisa has agreed to stay for at least a month.

John is as good as his word, and around midnight I head into the beach in pitch darkness to pick him up along with two companions, Richard and Sarah. It's like some clandestine drug deal as they flash a torch to indicate their position and I nose gently into the sand lifting the outboard so as not to hit the bottom, before loading them and a pile of bags into the inflatable.

The weather isn't looking great for getting into the Mediterranean. The chart shows persistent easterlies funnelling out of the straits of Gibraltar, like a gigantic fart, as Adam eloquently puts it. If we wait for the wind to become more favourable, we could be stuck in Cadiz for weeks and potentially end up at square one with no crew. It's better to push on. What we have in our favour is the current flowing east for much of the day.

To help make progress against the strong breeze, we motor sail with one engine as well as the reefed main and staysail. We tack close inshore watching the depth sounder like a hawk. This keeps us out of the strongest headwinds which are further offshore. When the depth gets below seven or eight metres, we tack back out again for half a mile before repeating the process. This way we zig zag slowly along the coast past dusty brown hills and white sandy beaches.

This method has a secondary benefit; it's less likely we'll encounter orcas. There has been a lot of press about a rogue pod of Iberian orcas attacking yachts along the southern coast of Spain and Portugal outside of the straits of Gibraltar. They focus on the rudder, gripping it in their mouths, worrying it like a dog, until it snaps off. There are websites mapping the encounters and over the past three years there have been hundreds of attacks. A small number of yachts have sunk, but no one has been killed so far. It's a mystery why the orcas are doing this, it's possibly some sort of game. Worryingly, the trend seems to be spreading as there have been some attacks as far north as the Bay of Biscay suggesting these orcas are passing on their knowledge to others. From the reports, they seem to prefer modern production yachts, with easily accessible spade rudders which reassures us a little, although the day before we leave Cadiz a Volvo 65 racing yacht is attacked going through the straits. We speculate it might be harder to pull off El Oro's rudder, but I'm reluctant to test the theory.

We don't see any orcas which is a little disappointing, although I'm pleased not to be attacked. We edge our way south past Cape Trafalgar and turn the corner to go east. We briefly consider unscrewing Nelson's decanter from its holder so we can toast the great man as we pass the site of his most famous victory. However, we're heeled over in the fresh breeze and have a bit on, so I'm reluctant to risk getting it out. It's also 11.00 in the morning so we raise our coffee cups in deference.

Off Tarifa we sail into a swarm of kite surfers. Their brightly coloured kites dipping and lifting in jerky motion. They're like a cloud of small insects that parts as we approach. I'm worried one will collide with us tangling their gear around our rig, but they fly past confidently. Some even take their hand off the control bar to wave to us.

In the afternoon, we lose the advantage of the current and our progress slows. We can see the coast of North Africa now, a few miles to the south. It's brown and arid through the heat haze. A distant line of ships tracks parallel with the coast, dirty black smoke indicating their presence. We continue to tack back and forth, each zig zag moving us a couple of miles further on and by mid-afternoon we make it around the corner. The wind dies, and we motor into the vast Bay of Gibraltar.

It's scorching hot and the famous rock appears, shimmering out of the hazy smog. We make our way in flat calm through a series of anchored ships, tankers queueing for their turn to unload at the refinery. We pass a British naval vessel tied up against the quay and round a long low breakwater to drop anchor in La Conception de la Linea on the Spanish side of the border.

Roscoe leaves us having sailed all the way from Bermuda. He's booked a hire car to take him to Malaga and I take advantage of his wheels to try and get a replacement gas bottle for the stove. The hire car office is in Gibraltar airport, so he and I walk across the border from La Linea. We get our passports stamped leaving Spain and show them again a few metres further on going into Gibraltar. We walk the short distance to the airport and Roscoe does the paperwork for the car. It's parked back on the Spanish side however, so we get stamped back in. Once in the car we drive back into Gibraltar to find the chandlery. Our passports are stamped again. I'm going to need a bigger passport at this rate. We negotiate the one-way system around Gibraltar, which reminds me of Milton Keynes, and after a few attempts find someone who'll sell us a gas bottle. From there it's back to La Linea picking up a fourth stamp on the way.

We pick up Tom by dinghy and promptly leave him by himself to mind the boat while we go back ashore. He's never driven an outboard before, but he gamely drops us off on the breakwater and we walk back into Gibraltar (another stamp) to explore. The pedestrian route in involves crossing the runway and it's a bit surreal to walk across the vast tarmac expanse. There's a security guard whose job is to hold up pedestrians when an aircraft is landing or taking off. We wander around for a few hours trying to get a feel for the place. It's an odd mixture of old and new architecture crammed into a small space, and there are a lot of English voices. We trudge slowly up the rock. There's not much of a view as the haze is so thick. The heat defeats us, and we get halfway; a mangy looking barbary ape watching from a rock wall as we shuffle back down. We pass the ruins of the unclimbable fence. This is a metal structure erected in the early 1900s to deter walkers from climbing the rock. I'm pleased to read on the accompanying plaque that multiple climbers have taken that as a challenge and scaled both fence and rock.

Back in La Linea after a sixth stamp in my passport we try and call Tom to pick us up. We can't get any phone signal and the breakwater is 500 metres from the boat, so too far away to shout. Lou strips to her underwear and dives in. She's halfway back when Tom notices we're on shore and comes and gets us. He doesn't see Lou, buzzing straight past her and she's climbing out onto the boat when we return.

In the morning we leave early, making for Ibiza. We have new crew joining in Sardinia, but Ruth needs to leave before we get that far to catch a flight back to Australia. We consider trying to drop her on the Spanish mainland, perhaps in Alicante or Benidorm, but it makes more sense to try and get a bit further before stopping. The breeze gets up as we make our way through the busy shipping traffic outside Gibraltar. As well as the stream of cargo vessels going through the Straits, there are ferries crossing over from Europe to ports in North Africa and back again. We have a favourable wind from our quarter for the first eight hours and make steady progress along the coast. We pass Malaga but soon after the breeze swings round in front of us. It's not particularly strong but is right on the nose. We tack slowly back and forth along the Spanish coast; the white beaches crammed with sunbaking holidaymakers.

Behind them the ground rises steeply to a mountainous interior.

This corner of Spain seems particularly busy with shipping as tankers and container ships coming into the Mediterranean either push past to the east or branch up towards the north. During the day these give us an interesting distraction to look at, and we check out their details on the AIS. This shows their length in metres, their speed, destination and as well as how close they'll come to us, and when that will be. Some of these ships are enormous, at one stage we come close to a container ship 400 metres long. At night they become a bit more threatening; watching their lights, it can be confusing to work out if they will pass ahead or behind us. Several times when I'm off watch I'm woken up to be asked what we should do about an approaching vessel. We track their bearing on the AIS and if it remains constant, we're on a collision course and must take some evasive action.

Sarah and Richard, who we've never met before, and who joined us from the UK with about 12 hours' notice, are both recent retirees and determined to make the most of their newfound time. The day after they get off El Oro in Sardinia, they're flying to Greece on another sailing holiday. Richard worked in IT while Sarah had a career in the police and is a retired detective which elicits lots of questions. She worked for a while on Operation Yewtree, the investigation into the paedophile ring surrounding Jimmy Saville. We quiz her on this, hoping for some salacious celebrity gossip, but it's a depressing topic and would have been a tough area to work on. She is also the more forthright of the couple, and Richard is chivvied along throughout the day. As he has the same name as me, I flinch every time she calls out 'Richard.' She gives me a withering look. 'If I'm issuing instructions,' she says, 'they're for my husband. If it's a question, it's probably for you.'

JULY

SOMEWHERE OFF BENIDORM Louisa delivers the bad news that the forward head isn't working. The bowl is full to the brim so Lou and I bail it out using a tin can to decant the unpleasant contents into a bucket. John comes and joins us, and it becomes clear we'll need to dismantle the macerator pump to work out why it's stopped working. The problem is it's impossible to reach. There's a narrow opening behind the loo which is much too tight to access the pump bolted to the back of the porcelain bowl.

To get to it, we need to remove the whole loo. This seems a drastic step as it's firmly bolted and sealed to the hull, so I'm a little hesitant. An hour or so later we haven't come up with an alternative, so we attack the sealant with a stanley knife. It's rock hard and has been applied very thickly; we break several blades before eventually managing to prise the bowl off the wall. It's still connected to the holding tank, a metre or so above it, by a thick plastic hose. This hose is full of sewage which is going to gush out over me the moment I disconnect it. John gamely tries to syphon the contents of the hose into our bucket using another shorter plastic pipe but without much success. In the end I use a plastic bag to catch most of the contents but it's still a messy, smelly job.

Once we have the toilet free, we pull the whole thing out onto the deck and wash it with the deck hose. The pump is rusty and ridged with brown streaks of corrosion. We find the smallest spanner in our toolbox and undo the series of tiny nuts securing the cover. Underneath, we find the problem. There's a wet wipe tightly wrapped round the rotor. We clean it out and put everything together again, bolting the toilet back in place. It's taken the best part of a day to fix, but it's very satisfying to press the flush button and watch the water suck straight out of the bowl.

Later that afternoon we have the autopilot on as usual when the wind suddenly backs through 90 degrees. The big genoa is pressed aback, hard against the spreader. It takes a few moments to disconnect the autohelm and get back on track, but we sort things out and carry on. A little later Til glances upwards and spots what looks to be a hole in the genoa. It must have been caused by the end of the spreader. We're nervous it might spread further, ripping the sail in two, so we furl up the sail and use the staysail instead.

Our third night out from Gibraltar the wind finally relents and comes around to the north and we can lay a course direct for Ibiza. It's a shame we don't have the genoa in action as there's a perfect breeze, but we keep one engine ticking over to help the smaller staysail and main. Eventually out of the darkness we pick up the lighthouse marking the south-eastern tip of Ibiza and soon after there's the outline of the land silhouetted against the starry sky. It's about 4.00am when we creep into a quiet bay flanked by low cliffs. There's a large superyacht to one side, but otherwise it's empty and we drop our anchor around 200 metres from the shore. The water is so clear I can see the bottom six or seven metres below us in the moonlight.

In the morning, daylight reveals a wonderfully rugged landscape. The shoreline is rocky with a series of coves and behind these the ground rises arid and inhospitable. The tumble of rocks is interspersed with a few green shrubs and the occasional olive tree. There are some well-kept houses nestled amongst these although we see no signs of life.

We have a brief pit stop in Ibiza as we need to leave again in the evening if we're going to make Sardinia in time to meet flights out. Juggling travel arrangements for guests on the boat is difficult. People arrive on the boat, and they want some certainty about when and where they can get off. What guests don't initially understand is how much we are at the mercy of the weather. If the wind is against us, the trip will take longer and be more uncomfortable. If the wind is very strong, we may not be able to go at all. On El Oro we also have a lot of breakages which can impact our progress. We'll try our utmost to meet an agreed schedule but there's always risk around timing, something which can make people uncomfortable.

We drop Ruth ashore; she's flying out the next morning and books a night in a hotel near the airport. She's a bit uneasy about being abandoned on the rocky beach so Til and I stay with her until the taxi arrives. There's a simple beach shack restaurant a few metres back from the water's edge, the sort of place in the Caribbean we might have gone for a rum punch. 'It's drinks time somewhere,' says Til. 'I think I'll have a glass of wine while we wait.' She picks up a drinks list from the table and quickly puts it back. The wines shown are €600 a bottle. We have a beer instead.

It would be nice to spend some time here, but we make the most of our day, relaxing in the warm sunshine or doing a few jobs like repairing the broken slugs on the main. At one stage Tom accidentally drops his watch overboard and it sinks to the bottom. The water is so clear he's able to dive and retrieve it.

We leave that evening as planned and head east through the gap between Formentera and Ibiza. There's no wind and as we motor past Formentera in the golden evening light, we take evasive action to avoid a stream of motorboats heading across our path towards Ibiza. It's like crossing a major highway at rush hour and we're in some danger of getting tee boned.

Once through the highway of motorboats we're back on our own and the light soon fades. Later that night we spot the distant loom of Mallorca and afterwards there's nothing as we motor for 48hrs across a glassy flat sea. Our wake cuts through the expanse of water, as if causing a light furrow in the brow of some sleeping giant. Beads of sparkling phosphorescence tumble aside as the hull of the yacht pushes through the dark sea. The engines don't miss a beat, droning steadily at 1,500 revs pushing us forward at seven knots. At one stage an amber warning light flickers on the dash, but it's likely a faulty electrical connection, so we ignore it, and it disappears again.

It's about 330 miles from Ibiza to the southwestern tip of Sardinia and we are heartily sick of the roar of the engines by the time we get there. It stays windless almost all the way, the breeze finally springing to life as we close the shore. There's a promising looking bay called Cala di Guida on Isola St Pedro and we drop anchor there in the late afternoon two days out from Ibiza. It's heavenly to be able to swim and relax in peace and quiet.

We get going again in the morning motoring slowly around

the coast on our way to Cagliari. We pass the beautiful Isola di San Antonio and around the corner along the southern coast of Sardinia. There are enticing deep bays with sandy beaches and plenty of potential anchorages. It would be nice to revisit this area and spend some time exploring. At some point the wind springs up from behind us so we get some sail up. We've no sooner cleated off the halyards when the fickle breeze swings around 180 degrees right onto our nose. We drop the sails again and keep motoring. An Italian coast guard vessel gives us a close drive by. We haven't checked in anywhere, perhaps he's going to challenge us. He gives us a good stare but goes on his way. At midday we pass Cape Spartivento, the lighthouse marking the turning point north towards the capital. A little further up the coast we edge slowly past the tanks of a large oil refinery, gas flares burning from the tall chimneys and the faintest whiff of ethanol in the air. We dodge around the anchored ships waiting their turn to come into the long wharf. From there we leave the shore to cross a large bay, the city of Cagliari stretching up the hillside through the smog in the distance.

We've booked into a marina for a couple of nights as we need to find a sailmaker to repair the genoa. Portus Karalis is painfully expensive at €240 a night but it's also right in the heart of town so it's a convenient spot to stop. Tom leaves us the next morning taking a train to the airport and later that day Richard, Sarah and John also say goodbye. It's just Lou, Til and me on the boat for the next few days.

With the help of the marina staff, we find Riccardo, the sailmaker who can fix our genoa. It's going to take him a week, so we have some time to explore Cagliari and surrounds. We walk for miles; the city rises steeply behind the port, so we get plenty of exercise for our unfit legs. We have some trouble locating the art museum walking in circles around it, but we find it in the end enjoying the beautiful collection of Morandi drawings. In a narrow sloping laneway, we have the best pizza I've ever eaten in my life. The city is grimy and a bit down at heel, but it seems full of locals rather than tourists and it has a gritty authentic character; it's not putting on a show for anyone. Some years ago, Til and I went to Northern Sardinia with Ruth for a sailing holiday. We didn't end up doing much sailing as the mistral blew strongly all week, so we had an opportunity to explore onshore. The place seemed coiffured and manicured for visitors and was teeming with Russian oligarchs on superyachts. It was also hideously expensive. Cagliari and the south of Sardinia seems much more down to earth and I'm glad we made the decision to call in here.

With three of us on board we can't afford to spend long in the marina. We still have some time to kill before our next guests arrive and before we can pick up the genoa, so we head east to Geremeas, two hours from Cagliari. It's a shallow indent on the coastline which the Navily app suggests will be sheltered. In fact, it's the opposite. We roll all night and wake up to strong winds pushing us towards a lee shore.

It's calmer further along the coast and we spend a couple of pleasant days in a more sheltered cove called Torre Stella. There's an old tower on the point which must be an ancient navigational marker and which the place is presumably named after. The water is deep blue, and the bottom a mix of sand and sea grass. It's illegal to anchor on the seagrass as well as being impractical as the hook of the anchor often won't dig in through the mat of vegetation. The water is so clear you can see the bottom at around 10 metres, so we have a person on the bow when anchoring pointing out the sandy patches.

Two days later we're back in Cagliari. This time we anchor off Poetta beach on the eastern side of the city. We're there to pick up our next guests, Harriet and Jimmy. Til met these guys at a drinks party when she was in the UK while I was crossing the Atlantic. Gamely they agreed to join us and they're now on board for a couple of weeks, helping to bring the boat across to Corfu.

We have a few more days to kill, so we potter along the south-eastern coast ending up at Torre Stella once again. At one point we're hailed by a man in a dinghy who thinks we're Kriter, the famous sister ship to El Oro that came third in the first Whitbread round-the-world race. It turns out Kriter is now based in Sardinia and used for charter. Hopefully we'll see her somewhere.

Finally, I get the call from Riccardo the sailmaker and we agree to meet at Marina da Piccola, off Poetta. We go ashore in the dinghy and wrestle the huge sail into the inflatable. He's given me a deal for cash, and I hand up a wad of notes. He looks around furtively ushering me off the dock and out of sight behind his truck. 'The tax inspectors are everywhere,' he says. 'If they see me taking cash it could be very bad for me and for you.'

Riccardo has done a beautiful job on the sail and it's good to be able to hoist our big grey genoa once again. The boat powers up immediately and as we wind on the winch El Oro heels to the breeze and accelerates, the bow pushing the blue water aside. We do two long tacks to get to the eastern point of Sardinia and anchor there for the night and most of the next day waiting for a favourable wind to get us to Sicily. A heatwave is building and it's nearly 40 degrees in the middle of the day. We have our awning rigged, but the sun is unrelenting and it's hard to find shelter from the searing heat. We spend a lot of time in the water. Jimmy and Lou are both enthusiastic long-distance swimmers and they have swim club every morning before breakfast which involves heading off for some distant point. With their encouragement, I join them on a couple of occasions but am soon left far behind as they're much stronger swimmers. Jimmy is training for a swim from Albania to Corfu in a few weeks' time. He doesn't look much like a swimmer with his skinny arms, but he is a powerhouse in the water.

The breeze swings round to the southwest in the late afternoon and we pull up the anchor as the heat of the day is easing. Unusually for the Mediterranean we have the wind in our favour for the full 170-mile crossing. During the night it threatens to drop a few times but each time we think it's going to fade out it builds again, and we romp across to Sicily with a bone in our teeth. We regularly reach 10 kts surging through the darkness with the wind on our quarter. There's some weird radio traffic on the VHF which continues throughout the night. At one stage a spooky voice comes up on channel 16 saying in heavily accented English, 'I can see you.' There's a pause before it comes again, 'I can smell you...'

By dawn we're well over halfway across the channel and it continues to blow a steady 15 kts. Til produces her trademark breakfast of eggs, bacon and beans and not long after we spot the faint outline of high ground in the distance. The northwest of Sicily is mountainous, and it takes a long time to close the coast, but we eventually get to the town of San Vito lo Capo mid-afternoon — twenty-two hours after leaving Sardinia. The anchorage is tucked in behind a breakwater at the end of a long bay and it's crowded. We squeeze uncomfortably between a large motorboat and a rafted-up group of RIBs filled with noisy local boys sunbaking and fishing. We're crowding them slightly, but soon after most of them move off leaving us plenty of room.

The town is spectacularly positioned between a high range of mountains and the sea, and we go ashore to explore in the evening. It's also very popular, we are now in peak season, and it's full of tourists and the bars and restaurants are packed.

We wander around for a while jostling through the throng before finding a pizza place which slightly disappoints after our amazing experience in Cagliari.

There's no rest for the wicked, so we're away early in the morning pushing on to Cefalù, mid-way along the north coast of Sicily. It's flat calm once again so we motor a mile or so off the shore. The heat builds quickly, and we shelter beneath the awning as we pass Palermo in a haze of smog. The centre of the city is hidden in the murky air, but we see the houses spreading up the hillside behind. This is one of the few places where we come across lots of floating rubbish in the water. Plastic bags like jellyfish pulse in the current, a metre or two under the surface. The shoreline curves away in a gigantic bay and we cut the corner, losing sight of the land for a while before re-joining it late in the afternoon. The anchorage at Cefalù is a narrow strip of shallow water lying off the town. There's no real shelter, but this doesn't matter as there's no wind forecast. The city itself is beautiful and we come ashore into the tiny old harbour past a ruined archway looking north out to sea and walk into a labyrinth of small alley ways and ancient buildings. It's heaving with tourists and it's slow work pushing through the crowds. Eventually we get to the main square and have a drink under the magnificent Norman cathedral dominating the town.

We have a bit of a scare leaving the anchorage in the morning. We're tidying the anchor away motoring slowly off from the land when a man fishing from a small dinghy shouts at us in alarm, waving his arms. Underwater there's the outline of some large rocks, uncomfortably close. One of them is directly ahead a couple of metres below the surface and we narrowly avoid it. There's nothing at all shown on the GPS plotter but a later check on Navionics on my phone shows scattered rocks north of the town.

It's another scorching windless day and we motor offshore heading northeast for Lipari, one of the Aeolian islands. These are a group of volcanic islands sitting offshore from Sicily. They include Stromboli which is still active, regularly belching out smoke and fire. It's another long day motoring until the various islands appear one by one out of the haze. We first close the coast of Vulcano. From there we cross the narrow channel over to Lipari. The shoreline is dramatic with steep cliffs plunging into the sea. Dark slits in the cliffs suggest caves which could be explored later and there are also intriguing natural stone archways among the impressive rock formations. Anchoring is difficult as the cliffs continue under water and it's deep close inshore. We have a few goes to get our anchor secure but eventually get settled in a bay crowded with motorboats and other craft. As the afternoon wears on most of the other boats leave and by dusk we have the place almost to ourselves. We spend an enjoyable afternoon exploring in the dinghy, poking deep into the caves and checking out the various islets, driving through some of the rock archways. As the sun dips towards the western horizon, I go for a walk with Jimmy and Harriet into the interior to try and see across to the other side of the island. We wind upwards along a rough goat track higher and higher. The track meanders past tiny paddocks of olives carved out of the rocky hillside and we occasionally disappear into lush green thickets of bamboo. It's steep; blind summit follows blind summit, and the top seems elusive. Eventually, despairing of getting a clear view from the road, we push through some light security fencing and climb a steep driveway to a house under construction. It's evening and there's no one around so we brazenly walk up the steps to the upstairs veranda and from there have a perfect view over the east coast of Lipari and north to Stromboli.

Swim club in the morning is interrupted by the presence of

small brown stinging jellyfish. Jimmy makes a few attempts to head in different directions but is thwarted each time coming back with a series of unpleasant red weals across his body. We get going instead, heading through the channel between Lipari and Vulcano, the two islands rising high out of the flat water. Hydrofoil ferries come past at 35kts ducking in and out of the various ports in the islands like pollinating bees. It's hot and calm again and we push through an oily flat sea towards the straits of Messina.

There's a long sand spit at the north-eastern tip of Sicily and once we're past that, the sea turns deep blue and there are strange lines of disturbed water. The high ground of Calabria on the other side of the straits is a few miles away and we motor cautiously towards it through the disturbed water. The current picks us up and sweeps us south. I glance at the speed over ground on the GPS, up over 10 kts. After days of calm, a hot blast springs up from behind so we come round into it and hoist the sails. We are surrounded by swordfish boats. These traditional fishing boats have very high masts with two or three people clustered at the top perched as lookouts. They also have enormously long bowsprits, more than twice the length of the boat. A harpooner stands on the end of the bowsprit guided by the lookout. These brightly coloured vessels carve across the straits at pace looking for their quarry and we keep a close eye out to avoid getting in their way. Ferries cross from both sides of the straits adding to the traffic.

The breeze becomes fresh and with the favourable current we make quick progress. The channel widens out and we bear away towards Calabria. As we close the coast, we're engulfed by a swarm of kite surfers. The swarm parts around us and soon after we're around the corner of the toe of Italy heading east. It's a poor region with run down housing and grey volcanic beaches. There's no shelter from the south at all, fortunately the wind is from the north, or we would have trouble finding a place to stop for the night. On a couple of occasions, we come across blow up toys from the beach heading out to sea. An inflatable unicorn bobs past and later we see a pink swan on its way towards North Africa. We anchor off a quiet stretch of beach near another Capo Spartivento. There's a railway line that runs along the coast and every hour a two carriage train rattles past.

There's no respite from the heatwave and after a quiet night and the usual early morning swim marathon, we continue along the coast with our awning up trying to stay out of the searing sun. On the shoreline we pass some wrecked yachts flipped over like beached whales, their bellies exposed, keels dug into the sand. We speculate how they got there; it would be horrible to be here in a southerly blow. Yellow fire brigade planes swoop out of the sky and skim across the sea, scooping up water to fight bushfires further inland. We're a mile or two offshore, but a high-speed customs boat roars out from the land and circles tightly round us before heading back into shore again. Later a coastguard vessel does the same thing. I'm not sure what they're looking for, but they wave cheerily before heading off. The wind gets up in the afternoon and is strong and gusty; we're now in the Gulfo di Squallacci, and we romp along under genoa and mizzen at over nine knots. Harriet is at the helm and looks in her element. She last crossed the Mediterranean forty years earlier in a small yacht with her father. They travelled from the UK and came through the canals in France and out into the Med before going on to Turkey. They lived on board for months and she has plenty of stories of near disasters, running onto reefs and getting caught in storms.

Eventually in the late evening we get to our destination, the small township of Castello – but the wind has shifted and it's not a safe spot to stop. We consult Navily which has a few suggestions further around the corner, but the potential anchorages are rocky and I'm not comfortable stopping. Finally, after the sun has dropped behind the land and the light is fading, we come to place called Capo Bianco which is more sheltered and has some large sandy patches we can still make out in the twilight. We drop our anchor in one of these patches and come to a rest in around 4 metres of water.

It's been a long couple of days and we're keen to get to land so we drop the dinghy in and buzz ashore. There's no quaint Italian village to explore, rather we've landed in some strange resort or perhaps it's some sort of old people's home. We walk up the path from the beach and find ourselves in a fenced off area with artificial, slightly padded, blue flooring, like the base for an outdoor tennis court. Behind are what look to be a series of apartment blocks, but we don't see any people. In the fenced off area, we are alone apart from a bored looking bartender sucking on a cigarette behind a bar. We try and engage him in conversation, but he speaks no English, and our basic Italian doesn't get us very far. We enjoy a beer however as the last of the light fades and the day finally cools.

There's some discussion about trying to get to Puglia at the heel of Italy but looking at the chart there don't seem to be much in the way of sheltered anchorages on our route. We're also running short of time to get Harriet and Jimmy on a flight home, so it makes more sense to go direct to Corfu, about 130 miles away. The weather is predictably hot and calm, and we motor through the daylight hours and into the night. It's an uneventful crossing and we hardly spot any shipping. There's a bit of confusion to the watch schedule as none of us has realised there's a clock change between Italy and Greece but we sight the dark outline of Corfu around 3.00am. There's a series of islands and rocky shoals on the north-western tip of Corfu and we give these a wide berth. We close the coast as the first rays of golden light appear from behind the hills of Albania and drop anchor in a secluded bay to the east of Kassiopi.

Kassiopi is a classically charming Greek fishing village now more geared towards wealthy holidaymakers. It's centred around a horseshoe shaped harbour, the concrete wharf lined with a mix of brightly painted traditional fishing boats, visiting charter yachts and rental craft. There are several tavernas on the waterfront, blue and white checked tablecloths fluttering in the breeze, and everywhere we hear English voices. Behind the harbour the neat old town dissolves into a ragged series of laneways lined with shops and bars and a more modern architectural mix.

Back on the boat that afternoon, Lou gets the party started with a round of negronis. It's not long before we're dancing on the deck. The Greek islands are as far east as we're going, and the culmination of a very long voyage. From Portimão, where we joined the European mainland a month before, Til and I have sailed close to 2,000 miles with a series of inexperienced crew. The weather's been kind to us, but it's still hugely satisfying to have made it so far. We dance well into the night until the speaker runs out of battery which must be a relief to the yachts at anchor around us.

Next day we motor around the island to Corfu old town and anchor under the fort guarding the entrance to the bay. To sail in Greece, you pay a cruising tax called TEPIA which must be lodged online. The system is not intuitive, and the form is partially in Greek, and I defer to various online forums to work out how to complete it. In the end I almost get it right but snatch defeat from the jaws of victory by idiotically not linking my payment with the reference number. I realise my mistake as soon as I've pressed pay, but it's too late. I call my bank in Australia to try and stop the transfer going through, but they have 'unusually high call volumes' and I'm on hold for twenty minutes before getting through, to be told there's nothing I can do about it.

Leaving the others on the boat, I go off and see the port authorities to check in. In the port police office, there's a fierce looking woman wearing an impressive set of gold epaulettes. She scowls at me, pointing to a notice board when I ask what I need to do, barking instructions in Greek which doesn't help much. Eventually I comprehend she's asking why my TEPIA isn't paid. I try to explain I've paid it but without the right reference number. I may as well be explaining to a brick wall. She goes back to whatever she was doing at her desk, doing her best to make me go away, but I play dumb and don't move and she eventually sighs and looks up at me. I show her proof of the bank transfer and she despatches me to another office to pay a €15 fee. I'm not sure what this is for, but it's a good sign as it means things are moving. After more forms and some stamping of documents, she tells me in broken English to go to the customs office to get my transit log and afterwards go to the other end of the port to immigration before returning to her office. I'm a bit sceptical about needing to see immigration as we've come from Italy, but I don't argue with her. 'Should I do this today?' I ask, noting the sign over the door indicating the office shuts at 2.00pm and it's now 1.55pm. 'Yes, go now. Quickly!' She points me out the door.

In the customs office there are more forms to complete and more questions. They want to know where's my authority to skipper the boat. This hasn't come up before in any of the other countries I've visited, and I don't have this documentation. I message Kent to help. He's with Tim on Four Seasons, Tim's other boat, and they are on their way from Venice coming to Corfu in a few days' time. He says he'll ask Tim to send through a letter of authority. It won't come today however, as they're about to head offshore out of mobile range. I explain this to the customs lady promising I will email it to her. She frowns and mutters something under her breath but continues. The next problem is the TEPIA again. They look it up in the system and of course it's showing as unpaid as my payment hasn't linked to the application. This time, rather than trying to explain I stuffed up the reference, I show her the bank transfer confirmation and say the payment was made from an Australian bank so will take some time to come through. This does the trick and after an intense discussion with her superior she tells me to wait on a chair across the hall while they process the paperwork. It takes some time, but she eventually produces a transit log for us. With it safely in my hand I'm directed to another booth further along the corridor, pay €45 and the log is duly stamped.

From there it's off to the immigration department – the other end of the dock behind the cruise ship terminal. This is heaving with people catching ferries to Albania and there are long, slow queues behind all the desks. Worried I'm going to be there for hours, I manage to collar a passing official explaining I've come by yacht from Italy. She looks at me a little perplexed and tells me I don't need to see immigration as I've come from a port within the Schengen region. Triumphantly, I head back to the scary woman at the port police office and proffer my transit log; she can give me a final stamp and I can be on my way. Unfortunately, it's not so easy as she again complains the TEPIA hasn't been paid and we go round in circles once more. She seems at a loss as to what to do and as the offices are closing for the afternoon she finally relents and stamps my transit log telling me I must email proof of the paid TEPIA once the confirmation comes through. It's taken most of the day, but I'm finally good to go.

We stay anchored under the fort for a few days. It's a beautiful spot and a short walk into the old town. Once through the labyrinth of touristy laneways there are all sorts of useful shops. There's a great local market selling fruit and vegetables as well as fish of all shapes and sizes. We take a bag of dirty washing into town and find a laundrette. There's a barber next door and while my clothes are tumbling around their wash cycle, I have a haircut and shave. I'm a bit embarrassed and sorry for the barber, my hair hasn't been washed for a couple of months and the day is 40 degrees, so it's a hot sweaty mess.

Before saying goodbye to Jimmy and Harriet we tramp around the fort together. Originally built by the Venetians to defend the city, it's been added to by the British who controlled Corfu for much of the 1800s. We clamber over the stone ramparts and take the long winding path to the lookout at the top. The view is spectacular, but the hills to the north are shrouded in smoke streaking out across the water towards Albania. That evening we get texts from the fire authorities advising of dangerous bushfires with evacuation orders for several locations.

Lou goes the next day. She has been with us for a month since leaving Cadiz and we've enjoyed having her on board. Although not an experienced sailor, her energy and enthusiasm have been infectious, and she has embraced our mantra of trying to bring your best self to the boat, although she and Ruth both agreed that their worst selves could be much more fun. We're going to miss her. I help load her bag into the dinghy at 5.00am the next morning and we motor slowly in the dark through the moat that separates the fort from the old city. When we emerge on the north side, we both gasp at the view. The hillside across the bay is ablaze; it's glowing orange and along the skyline are leaping flames, towers of sparks spiralling into the darkness. We turn away and motor round to the ferry wharf where I drop Lou at the concrete mole between two ships, like a clandestine people smuggler.

Til and I enjoy a few hours to ourselves to visit the market and do a quick shop before Charlie, Charlotte & their son Milo appear on the dock having flown in direct from Newcastle. It's 40 degrees in Corfu and they're dressed for the northern English summer. It doesn't take much persuasion to get them to strip off and leap into the water.

Later, we pull up the anchor and motor ten miles south to Pretiti. The bottom there is mud, so the water isn't crystal clear, but it's a lovely old style Greek village with a small breakwater sheltering some fishing boats and a couple of simple tavernas on the beach. There's no wind and it's oppressively hot with smoke haze. Ashore we head into the quieter looking taverna, empty apart from an elderly Greek lady. She smiles at us, one surviving tooth prominent in an empty set of gums. She turns out to be the proprietor and her family has run the inn for over 100 years. She tells us it was started by her grandfather's father early in the last century. It doesn't appear to have changed very much in the intervening time, a simple sloped roof over a concrete floor.

After a couple of nights, we make our way north again and this time anchor around the far side of the fort outside the Mandraki marina. The sandstone conservatorium of music towers above us and we can hear the students practicing, the music carrying over the water. We push further north, anchoring in Ormos Kalami, a deep indentation in the narrowing channel between northern Corfu and Albania. There are a few yachts there already when we arrive, and the bay slopes steeply making it hard to find secure holding. We have a couple of attempts at anchoring and at one stage are asked to move by the water sports business who is doing a roaring trade in water-skiing lessons. Milo joins of one of these and we enjoy watching him progress from holding the fixed bar on the side of the launch to a double ski tow. Milo is fifteen and chattier than most teenagers of that age; if he minds being dragged along on holidays by his parents, he doesn't show it. He's obsessed by all things military and is a walking encyclopedia about tanks and weapons. He tells us he wants to join the marines when he leaves school. It's good to have some young muscles on board to help with the heavy jobs on the boat.

We eventually find good holding on the southern side of the bay across from the White House, a restaurant on the beach that was once the Durrell's house. We're next to a cruising yacht with a mixed Swedish Australian family including some small kids – a baby and a five-year-old. They have their Australian in-laws on board, who reveal they keep their boat at the Royal Motor Yacht Club in Newport very close to where we used to live. It's a small world.

It's a good thing we're well anchored as the next day the wind rises sharply and before long it's blowing twenty-five knots. The busy little anchorage becomes chaotic with boats dragging anchor and there's lots of shouting and gesticulating. There's an Italian catamaran which cannot get settled and re-anchors again and again, each time ending up closer than ever to another moored yacht. A small charter yacht comes in and anchors in front of us and the crew decamp ashore to lunch at the White House. Shortly afterwards we look up to see this boat bearing down on us with no-one at home. We rush to grab fenders but are unable to avoid it striking a glancing blow to our hull as it drifts backwards out to sea, the anchor chain dangling useless from the bow. I'm tempted to let it go on its way, but after having seen our neighbour leap in, swimming for it, Charlie and I launch the dinghy and chase after it. We are trying to work out how to start the engine and get the anchor back on board when the yacht's skipper arrives in his dinghy very flustered. It must have been disconcerting to glance up from lunch to see his vessel heading out to sea. Later he comes round to El Oro with a couple of bottles of wine to apologise for the drama. He's English and is embarrassed by the incident, but it could have been much worse. There isn't much damage to El Oro; a graze which polishes out and a slight chip in the paintwork. An hour later another yacht almost does the same thing missing us by inches. The crew are on board this time but have lost control of their vessel which drags out to sea. They don't return to the bay.

After two nights in Kalami the wind drops and we make our way south again to Corfu town stopping at Vido Island, half a mile north of the port. The island is surrounded by crystal clear water, rocky outcrops fringing small sandy coves. Inland, there are several walking tracks heading into the bush. I take a promising looking trail winding through the trees towards the centre of the island. The scent of pine needles heavy in the air, and with the buzz of cicadas it's like a magical lost world until I come across a huge pile of rubbish in a clearing in an overflowing skip. I can't imagine how this can ever be emptied as there doesn't seem to be a landing dock. Behind the skip is a high retaining wall with several doors into small cell like rooms that lead nowhere. Further along the track there's an old house that is derelict. It's an imposing building with a beautiful aspect looking south towards the old town. It would have been magnificent when it was in commission but now is a ruin. The front door is open and there's nothing to stop me entering, except the fear I'll fall through the floor, or the ceiling may collapse on my head.

Further on there are several old buildings mostly in disrepair and finally some signs of life. There are some tents and a makeshift recreational area; it appears to be a scout camp or perhaps a religious retreat. The island has a strange atmosphere and it's something of a relief to find my way back to the beach. Later we google it and find it has a chequered history. During the war it was used as a medical facility and so many patients died there was no room on the island for their corpses. They had to be buried at sea, their bodies weighted with rocks. The island was also used as a borstal; perhaps the cells I'd seen were used for that purpose.

In the evening we raise the anchor and motor the short distance to Corfu town. As we clear the western end of Vido Island, we spot a distinctive red hulled yacht heading the same way as us. We gradually close with it, and we recognise it as Four Seasons with Tim, Sophie, Kent and Randel on board. It's an emotional moment as Tim hasn't seen El Oro for nearly four years and we circle each other admiringly before dropping anchor in front of Mandraki port. The moment is slightly marred when the bolt in our anchor winch shears as we try and drop the chain. The chain runs out OK, but we know we'll have to pull it up manually if we can't replace the bolt.

We briefly go aboard Four Seasons and say hello properly, but Tim and Sophie are tired having sailed direct from Croatia and we're concerned about our anchor, so we plan to catch up the next day. Back on-board, Charlie and I dismantle the windlass, the first time I've taken it apart since we bolted the winch drum to the drive shaft in March. It's difficult to dismantle as the parts are stuck together with a combination of dried grease and salt. Some lubricant and a hammer do the trick. The stainless-steel bolt has sheared in two places and fortunately we find a spare of the same diameter. It's a fiddle to line everything up, but after some swearing and a few false starts we have a working windless once more. To prove to ourselves it works, and because we're not quite happy with our current anchorage, we pull up the anchor and motor around to the other side of the fort for the night.

We say goodbye to Charlie, Charlotte and Milo the next morning after spending an amusing forty-five minutes watching a superyacht trying to get off the dock. Unfortunately, its neighbour, another massive powerboat has laid its anchor chain over theirs, a common occurrence, and it is now in a tangle. Drifting helplessly a few metres off the dock they deploy their tender, itself half the size of El Oro, and the captain issues instructions over a handheld VHF. It takes a while, and there's a lot of prodding with boathooks, but eventually they take the weight off the neighbour's chain, and they can pull theirs free. Once they're gone, we take the boat around to Kommeno bay outside of Gouvia marina. Four Seasons is anchored there and after dropping our hook we head ashore with them in our tender. They have organised an expedition to Doukades, a small village high in the hills of northern Corfu. We have an ouzo in the village square while waiting for Tim's friends, Mark and Julie who turn up twenty minutes later with their daughter Charlie. Mark is a retired Colonel who previously commanded the Gurkha Regiment. He is tall and fit looking and far from the stereotypical retired Colonel. His wife Julie is a high-ranking secret agent, according to Tim. We're not sure what she does but she's fun and full of energy and she tells us she's off to Kyiv in the morning on some government business. They live for half of the year on a beautifully restored motor yacht called Wild Venture which they keep in Gouvia marina.

They've organised a hike for us prior to dinner which seems ambitious given we've two octogenarians in our party. Nevertheless, we meander slowly up an old donkey track to the top of the line of hills keeping a weather eye out for their dog, a young fluffy Alsatian with a penchant for picking up rocks and huge sticks, ideal for catching the unwary on the legs. Eventually we emerge on the ridgeline by a tiny, whitewashed church on the edge of a cliff looking out across the western shore of Corfu. The setting is dramatic with precipitous drops beneath us and a stunning view to the little port at

Palaiokastritsa. Mark opens his rucksack and produces a bottle of rose and several cold beers which are extremely welcome.

We head back down the hill into the dusk and make our way to the village and dinner in Elisabeth taverna. The restaurant there is run by a Belgian émigré, and we are made to feel very at home tucking into rabbit stifado. There's a fiesta in the town and when we leave, well after midnight, the party is just getting started.

Tim and Sophie invite us out for a day on Four Seasons. It seems strange to leave El Oro unattended, but we put our faith in the anchor to look after her while we're away. Four Seasons is a very comfortable boat, about the same length as El Oro but a sloop and a bit beamier. She is in immaculate condition and the varnished woodwork looks stunning. She's more modern than El Oro and we admire, with a little envy, the large electric self-tailing winches as well as the state-of-the-art Italian coffee machine in the galley.

Kent motors the boat up to Kouloura and we spend a pleasant day anchored off the cove. It's very relaxing to be on a boat and not be responsible for it. Bar Pegna, an old friend of Tim & Sophie is also aboard; she joined the previous evening. She's been cruising with them for years and when I ask how long she'll be on the boat, she says, 'I haven't booked a ticket home. I'll stay until they're bored with me.' She's sparky and quick witted and we enjoy her company. Tim cooks up a beautiful lunch; lamb and roast vegetables and we have a few drinks under the awning on the aft deck.

In the evening they head into the marina at Gouvia as they have the rigger booked for the next day. We go back around to Corfu old town once again – we're meeting Evie and Jai who fly in from London. They're our first repeat customers; back on the boat some seven months after staying with us in the Caribbean. Once the kids have arrived, we motor back round to Gouvia; we're keen to catch up with the Four Seasons crew once more. We anchor in the bay outside of the marina in a very similar place to where we had left the boat before. There's no wind and there seems little risk as we head into the marina in the dinghy. Ashore we meet our friends, joining them in the marina pool where there's a little restaurant and we have lunch.

In typical Ionian fashion the breeze builds after lunch and I'm uncomfortable we can't see the boat from where we're sitting. Napkins blow off the tables in the restaurant and the large shade cloths strain against their ties. At one stage Tim mentions he once had trouble with the holding in the bay where we're anchored, skidding across the seagrass. I don't know if this was a deliberate prompt, but I take the opportunity to make some hasty apologies to my lunch companions and run to the end of the pontoon. At first, I can't see El Oro, but after some searching, I spot her across the bay. A moment's relief and then a realisation she's not where we left her. I leap into the dinghy and ignoring the 4-knot speed limit, carve a wake through the marina entrance and out of the channel.

Miraculously she hasn't hit anything, but she has dragged a couple of hundred metres. Our track on the plotter is instructive showing a steady line to the southeast. There was a large power boat behind us when we anchored which she must have narrowly missed as well as a rocky breakwater. We're sitting stopped for the time being on a shallower patch in about 5 metres of water but I've no confidence we're properly dug in. I bring the anchor up and motor to the far side of the bay out of the wind and I've just re-anchored when Kent arrives with Til and the kids on board the Four Seasons tender. He's very nice about the fact we've dragged halfway across the bay, and we file this experience in our 'miss is as good as a mile' locker.

AUGUST

In the morning we're joined by Maddy, the daughter of some close friends. Like Evie and Jai, she too has recently moved to London from Sydney, and will be with us for a week. We stock up on some provisions before heading south for Paxos. Most days a gentle north westerly breeze sets in during the afternoon, but today we have a light southerly, so we motor. It's around four hours from Corfu town and we get to Lakka at the northern end of the island shortly before dusk. It's a perfect natural harbour, a deep inlet with a ninety-degree bend and a small village at the head. The water is crystal clear and in the sunshine it's a perfect turquoise. It's also very crowded. We nose into the bay weaving our way through the thicket of anchored yachts. There's no space inside, so with difficulty we turn around and head out again. There's some room close to the entrance next to a large superyacht — the motor variety. It's our first attempt at taking lines ashore and we make a hash of it. We drop the anchor alright and Maddy and Evie try to swim ashore with the lines. They get in a tangle and the wind catches the boat, so it drifts away from the shore. By the time the girls get anywhere near the rocks we've run out of rope and we're frantically tying new sections on. Our rope also doesn't float; our more experienced neighbours have large reels of bright yellow floating polyester line, and at one stage our line catches on the seabed becoming jammed. Evie dives to free it and eventually we get a loop onto a rock. It's a long hard pull to get the boat secured and we are all ready for a beer by the time we are snuggly set. It's worth the effort however, as the bay is delightful, and the township is charming. The kids go in for drinks ashore and we later join them for cocktails at a bar on the water.

After a calm night, we detach ourselves from the rocks and head on south. We look in at Longos – Kent and Tim recommended we visit this bay. It's pretty but there's an onshore breeze and it looks choppy and uncomfortable. A couple of miles further on we see a large ferry disappearing into the shoreline, entering the hidden opening to Gaios. We follow it in, and the waterway becomes a narrow river leading to a bustling little town. The river is lined by yachts, and we find a spot on the eastern shore tying up to a wizened tree on one flank and a protruding rock on the other.

It's busy and there is a continual flow of boats coming and going. There are large tourist boats that skilfully navigate the narrow waterway as well as numerous yachts heading through to the town. As the afternoon draws on, the situation becomes farcical as vessels compete for fewer and fewer remaining berths. Yachts tie up to the most unlikely looking places which have been written off as untenable earlier in the day. When a large tourist boat comes and tries to moor, only to be blocked by several circling catamarans, there is predictable handwaving and shouting. It's a great spectator sport for those of us safely moored up.

Til and I go to try and get our transit log stamped. We're looking for the port police when they find us. Til is puttering along in the dinghy, but apparently going too fast and we're summoned to the shore by an angry official. We get a good telling off; at one stage during his rant, he shouts at us, 'I should pull you in to the office for two hours of processing…' Til apologises and he calms down, so I take the opportunity to ask him where I find the port police. 'Here of course' he says pointing to himself.

'Can you please stamp our Transit Log?'

'Where have you come from,' he asks.

'Corfu'

'And where are you going next?'

'Back to Corfu'.

'In that case,' he says, turning to walk away, 'you were never here.'

'But don't we need to get the log stamped?'

'Go back to your boat now!'

Sometimes Greek officialdom can be hard to fathom.

The following morning, we watch the exodus of yachts from the river. Some have anchor chains caught up with boats from the other bank and there's a lot of poking with boat hooks and pulling and pushing to get free. Fortunately, there's no wind and eventually the throng clears. We head out the way we came in and turn south once again, this time bound for Anti Paxos. It's a couple of miles away – a low island with enticing rocky coves and sandy beaches. The water over the sand almost defies description. The colour is so vibrant, the turquoise so bright, from a distance the yachts glow blue.

We are getting more practised now at our stern-to mooring and despatch the kids overboard with the lines, paying out the rope from the back of the boat. They get them fixed to the rocks without a hiccup and we're soon securely moored in a quiet cove near the southern end of the island. It becomes busier during the day as others join us, but it's still less frenetic than the anchorages on Paxos.

After a lazy day swimming and sunbaking we return to Paxos for the evening. We've had a message from Tim; he's in Longos and he's asked us to join him for dinner to celebrate his 83rd birthday. We find Four Seasons tucked in with lines ashore behind the outer breakwater and we squeeze in next to them putting a line between us so no-one else is tempted to fit in that gap. Ashore we drop the kids off at the Roxy bar and head to Vassilis' place, one of the original restaurants in the small town. Tim and Sophie tell us they used to come here in the 1970s and the place is still run by the same family. It's a fun night and they reminisce about their travels in the region 50 years before.

We go for a walk with Tim the next morning up the hill above the town. There's the ruin of an old windmill above the bay and we scramble up to look out on the two boats moored together. We follow the winding road further up the hill past some old, terraced farms and unkempt olive groves. From time to time there is some half-hearted development; some new villas which seems to have stopped mid-way through construction. Eventually we get to a church near the top of the hill and it's interesting to poke around the graveyard looking at the inscriptions on the mausoleums. There's a narrow winding path back and we're negotiating this when both the soles come off Tim's hiking boots. He finishes the walk in his socks joking he's left his soul in Paxos.

It has been very special to spend time with Tim and Sophie

after having sailed their boat for so long and it's sad when we part that afternoon. They circle El Oro as we sail north, taking pictures from every angle. They are heading to Albania to collect a sail which has been delivered there whilst we need to get back to Corfu town to pick up new guests.

Our plan is to spend the night off Boukari to save having to go all the way back to Corfu town in one day. The wind dies so we drop the sails, motoring slowly up the coast. We track parallel with the long sandspit that runs up from the southern tip of the island keeping to the 20-metre line about a third of a mile offshore. It's not far enough; late in the evening there's a bump and a moment later we squelch to a halt. Bemused we look at the chart – we're apparently in deep water well out in the 'safe' white area. There is no hint of shallow water on the plotter, but we're stuck hard aground. I put the engines into reverse, but we don't move. We try forward with the same result. There's a light offshore breeze so we try rolling out the headsail to see if we can induce any heel and pull the bow round, but still no movement. I pull out my phone to look at the Navionics app to see if there's any tidal information but there's nothing. We could be stuck for some time. What I do notice on the Navionics chart, however, are some user annotations saying the sonar soundings are wrong and the depths are shallower than shown.

We drop the dinghy into the water and first try to pull the bow round. There's still no movement so I pull backwards whilst Til guns both main engines in reverse. There's a shudder, and a moment later the boat is free, sliding back into deep water. Chastened, we head well offshore and give the end of the sandspit a wide berth before dropping anchor at sunset off Boukari.

The next day there's a change in the weather. It's overcast and humid and the forecast predicts thunderstorms. We head north to anchor in our favourite spot under the fort as the sky turns black. We pick up our next guest, Megan, before the heavens open, but I get caught dropping the kids ashore as the downpour breaks. There's strong wind with the storm and when I get back to the boat Til has the engines on as a precaution against the anchor dragging. In the end we don't need them, but several other boats drag past us heading out to sea.

Megan is from Victoria, and we became friends with her and her husband Ian when we lived in Melbourne twenty years ago. She has triplet boys and was over in Europe to meet them for a brief holiday in Germany before joining us for a few days. It's fun to catch up and reminisce about old friends.

The storm brings torrential rain, and the dinghy is soon full of water. In the morning the system has passed over, it's cooler and the air is sharp and clear as if cleaned by the rain. I paddleboard through the moat behind the fort where local fishermen are bailing out their craft.

After breakfast we head back around to Gouvia. Kent has organised Spiros to come and do a rigging check. Two of his guys, Andreas and Georges come round a little later and crawl all over the rig. Andreas is slight, whilst his companion is much larger, and it seems unfortunate to me the larger man is the one who must go up the mast. Andreas mutters a bit about our old-fashioned winches with no self-tailers and I help him to hoist Georges slowly up each mast. Of course, he finds a dangerous fault – a hairline crack in one of the mizzen cap shrouds so we organise to go into the marina to get it replaced the next day.

Whilst the guys are climbing the rigging, we have another crew change. Maddy leaves us; we're going to miss her swimming abilities when anchoring stern to. Shortly afterwards Til runs ashore in the dinghy to pick up Tom and Cath. Til shared a flat with Cath in London thirty years ago and although we haven't seen much of her since, they have kept in touch. She married Tom who's a bloodstock agent and they live near Newmarket, a long way from the sea. Their passions are horses and the country; staying on El Oro is well out of their comfort zone. Tom is a larger-than-life character in every way, and he regales us with stories of buying and selling multi-million-dollar stallions for Arab sheiks.

After a day in the marina where the riggers replace the damaged shroud we head back north once again, this time to Agios Stephanos. It's a snug little cove at the north-eastern tip of Corfu across the narrow channel from Albania. The harbour has no room, so we anchor stern to the rocks outside. We misjudge the distance from land and end up tying several lines together, leading them 100 metres to shore. The anchorage is deeper than I would like, around twenty metres, and while lowering the chain the bolt through the driveshaft sheers again. We continue to lower the chain manually until we have 75 metres out. It's going to be very heavy if we need to haul this in by hand.

Despite having our stern line marked with two large fenders, several small hire boats coming out from the harbour try to cut inside us. One of them goes straight over the top of our line; miraculously avoiding getting it caught in their propellor. Several others almost garotte themselves before turning back at the last minute. This set-up is too dangerous, so we release ourselves from the rocks and swing at anchor to the wind.

The girls run ashore and explore the little town before finding a taverna and settling in for a gin and tonic or two. Tom and I stay aboard and work on the windlass. It's difficult as we don't have the right sized bolt and we have to redrill the hole, but eventually, after some encouragement with the hammer, we finally slot the new one in and lock it off with a couple of nuts. The windlass gives us no more trouble for the rest of the trip.

After a quiet night we sail gently south again back to Corfu old town where we farewell all our guests, before spending a rare couple of days on board by ourselves. We take the boat round to Gouvia to pick up a replacement stainless-steel base plate for the halyard winch which Perm previously bent whilst hoisting the main with the strength of a gorilla. The new one is thicker and highly polished, and I can see the reflection of a bearded old man as I rivet it back onto the mast.

We knock off a few jobs while things are quiet including servicing all three engines. I'm slightly horrified at the state of the primary fuel filter; it's covered in sludgy grey sediment from the tanks, and it seems miraculous the engines have continued to run without a problem. The secondary filters have been doing their job.

Our brief period of alone time comes to an end all too soon and we meet our next guests on 14 August. Ross, an old friend from work, has flown out from Sydney to join us for the final few weeks. Also joining from London are Annabel and Martin. Martin runs a high-end travel business organising boutique guided tours to all sorts of places. He's very knowledgeable about the region and we're hopeful some of this might rub off on us. None of the new arrivals are experienced sailors, but they're all enthusiastic.

They arrive at lunch time and after a quick swim we take the afternoon northerly breeze and head south for Paxos. We do the twenty miles at a leisurely pace taking care to steer well clear of the sandspit at the southern end of Corfu. In the late afternoon light, we glide past Lakka and on to Longos where we tie stern to the rocks in the same spot where we moored a few weeks earlier with Four Seasons. It's the first experience of stern to mooring for the new crew and fortunately the breeze is light. Ross and Annabel take the lines ashore, and we secure ourselves competently next to a huge superyacht called King Louis.

We don't dwell in Paxos as we want to get to the Inland Sea, so after a morning ashore, we continue southwards. It's thirty-five miles to Lefkas, there's a building northerly breeze and we get there by early evening. Lefkas isn't technically an island; it's connected to the mainland by a swamp and centuries ago a narrow ship canal was dredged to allow access into the Inland Sea. The entrance to the canal is via a swing bridge that opens on the hour for vessels to move north and south through the waterway. We try to time our approach for opening time but get there a bit early. There is already a queue of yachts waiting in the confined space to the north of the bridge and in the strong afternoon breeze it's tricky to stay in the centre of the channel and avoid hitting the boat in front. There's also a current running adding to the difficulty. We're not the only boat having this challenge and there's a bit of shouting and arm waving before finally we hear the siren and the bridge swings open. With pent up energy, a stream of boats rushes out both north and south.

We follow the line of boats heading south, one behind the other moving at an orderly five knots through the canal. The landscape beyond the banks of the canal is flooded with low dykes and interspersed with strange, rusted metal wrecks. In the distance out to sea a swarm of kite surfers are gyrating dots. They remind me of school chemistry lessons; unconstrained molecules swarming about in a heated vessel. The canal gradually widens, and we are spat out in a nicely sheltered piece of water across from the town of Ligia. We anchor in perfect calm two hundred metres off the beach in good holding.

Ligia is not the most exciting town we've visited. There's a small harbour with a few fishing boats and an array of wooden dinghies moored fore and aft. A couple of tavernas sit back from the shoreline in front of a busy road. There's a smattering of shops along the road but there isn't much of a town centre. Getting out of the dinghy as we come ashore, Martin, who is gangly and a little uncoordinated, almost falls in the water but spectacularly saves himself with an impressive acrobatic manoeuvre.

The guest loo on board has stopped working again; this time the pump has died. This doesn't seem to worry Annabel and Martin. Annabel takes a bucket into their cabin at night and in the morning, we're amused to hear her instruct Martin to kindly deal with her chamber pot. Martin is a great storyteller and full of anecdotes. He has lots of interesting facts about people and places, but the best stories are about his business. At first glance he comes across as an intellectual – he could pass as an academic. In fact, he's an entrepreneur and a risk taker. Building his business from scratch has been a wild ride with all sorts of hair-raising risks along the way. Martin points to an anchored cruise liner, disgorging passengers into small orange lifeboats, telling us he previously rented it for one of his tours. It was a risky operation, the cost of renting the ship was huge, enough to send his business broke if they couldn't recoup the outlay with ticket sales. There were weeks of stress, but in the end the tour was a sell-out. He and Annabel have had a tough time during the covid years as the travel business came to an abrupt halt, but things have now bounced back strongly.

The high ground on Lefkas as we head south into the Inland Sea is mirrored by a series of distant peaks on the mainland and it's a spectacular view. We glide through flat water past the beautiful and secluded island of Skorpios, Onassis' private getaway. It's heavily wooded and has been well planned for privacy as the houses are difficult to spot from the water. Visitors are not welcome, there are large signs near the waterfront warning passing boats not to anchor, moor or even loiter.

We get to Meganisi and head into a deep bay at Spartochori for a look. We've been recommended to moor here but it doesn't look inviting, so we push on to a narrow inlet on the eastern side called Atheni Bay and anchor stern to shore. Til swims to shore and ties one of our lines to a telegraph pole. Hopefully the Greek electricity people don't mind.

Leaving Atheni we track back around the northern side of Meganisi and follow the coast southeast along a finger of rocky land. We've been told about a cave we should visit on our way through. It's easy to spot as there's a cluster of yachts hovering around the entrance. It's too deep to anchor so we leave Til and Martin on board while Ross, Annabel and I take the dinghy and check it out. We leave the dinghy at the entrance and swim in, it might be a bit dangerous to other swimmers if we drive into the dark cavernous space. Not everyone has that idea as we are almost run over by an enormous black and gold RIB which comes deep into the cave. A blond girl on the front in a leopard skin bikini clutches a small fluffy dog while a photographer snaps away.

We don't linger in the crowded cave, we want to get going for the little town of Kioni on Ithaka, a few hours away. The afternoon breeze springs up from the north and with the wind on our beam we race across the channel. We have the genoa and mizzen up as the main is hard to raise with a small crew, but El Oro loves this sort of breeze, and we power along at over eight knots. It's not rough, but the waves are building with the increasing wind. We're towing the dinghy behind us, which makes me nervous – in these conditions it should be up on the davits. The wind becomes stronger and the dinghy surfs down the waves catching us up for a moment before slowing and then jerking forward again. There's a real danger it could flip over which would be a disaster. It would be very hard to recover, and the engine would be ruined. It's too late now to do anything about it so I glance backwards and keep going.

Kioni is at the head of a dogleg bay on the north-eastern side of Ithaka. As we close the land the sea flattens out, but the wind remains disconcertingly strong, funnelling through the hills from the other side of the island. We motor into the bay unsure where we should anchor. The inner harbour is packed, and we discard that. Outside, there's a line of yachts moored stern to some cliffs on the southern side of the bay. We could join them, but it seems crowded, so we select the northern side, empty apart from one catamaran stern to the rocks.

This turns out to be a mistake. On the northern side, the seabed drops off steeply and it's difficult to get a good length of anchor chain far enough out to pull us clear from the shore. We have a couple of attempts at laying out the chain before sending Ross ashore in the dinghy with the lines. With some difficulty he attaches the first one to a rusty metal ring with a bowline. He's working on the second when a huge gust of wind catches us from the side. Our anchor drags sideways and our bow swings round towards the shore. Concerned we might end up on the rocks, I put the engine in gear and try and motor forward. The stern line becomes taut for a second; there's a bang and the cleat pulls clean out of the deck. It flies back and smashes into the large stainless-steel fairlead at the back of the boat and rips it from its mounting. Both expensive bits of hardware disappear over the stern and into the sea.

Freed from the restraining stern line we swing round on our anchor and lie parallel with the shore. We're in deep water and are comfortable enough for now, although it's not a safe anchorage. I call out to Ross, who's still in the dinghy at the shore, to retrieve the lines. Unfortunately, his bowline turns out to be some other sort of knot and it's very difficult to undo.

I pull on a mask and fins and swim over to help him. Eventually we manage to free up the tight knot and we heave the line back into the dinghy. In a stroke of good luck, Ross spots glints of metal on the seabed far below. They're our missing deck fittings and I take some deep breaths before diving to retrieve them. They're deep, well over ten metres, and I'm no free diver. I'm determined to get them however and after a couple of attempts, I surface with them in my hands.

Back on the boat we're discussing what we should do next after this disastrous attempt at mooring when we're hailed by two people in a small inflatable. They turn out to be some English friends, Richard and Tessa, who have chartered a yacht for a couple of weeks. They have a professional skipper with them, an easy-going young Dutchman called Thom. Thom points to their yacht, one of the ones moored stern-to on the southern side of the bay. 'Why don't you come and raft up next to us?' he says. There's a narrow gap between them and an Italian boat next door which I eye up dubiously. 'OK,' I say, 'but you'll have to help us in with your dinghy as I'm going to struggle going backwards in this crosswind.'

We set up to re anchor next to them which turns out to be difficult. Their outboard dies and won't restart so they're unable to help us in. As anticipated, the cross wind catches us, and we skew sideways, so I motor forward and try again. In all we make three attempts, the Italians on their small Beneteau looking increasing nervous with El Oro bearing down on them. They're suggesting maybe we should anchor somewhere else, when finally, we get a line ashore behind us and we're able to straighten up. From there we get settled and raft up with our friend's yacht, although it turns out we're not out of the woods yet. The wind continues to rise into the evening and some of the boats upwind of us swing sideways, putting pressure on their neighbours. A huge gold coloured superyacht drags and there's a lot of swearing and commotion as he pulls out of the anchorage leaving a trail of destruction in his wake. Thom confides he only has 25 metres of chain out and I'm also nervous I don't have enough to properly hold us both. We need to reset both anchors using our dinghy to drop out more chain. It works well and we even recruit the Italians, who, resigned to having us as neighbours have now cheered up. They use their dinghy to keep El Oro steady in the wind whilst we pull out 60M of chain and redrop the anchor from the back of our inflatable. On the hillside above us, an elderly Greek lady sits silently on her balcony surveying the chaos below.

After all that excitement it's a relief to be able to relax with a beer. Richard and Tessa have some friends aboard and they head ashore for the evening, but we stay on the boat and have Thom to dinner. He's worked for Sunsail for a few months but is already restless and looking for the next opportunity. Prior to covid he ran his own kite surfing school in South Africa but moved back to Europe to be closer to his family. He enthuses about El Oro and the opportunities Til and I could have managing yachts if we want that life. Til and I glance at each other. We're not sure we do.

After our stressful experience in Kioni, we determine to go somewhere easier to moor and Thom suggests we try Vathi a little further along the coast. It's the largest town on Ithaka and sits at the end of a long narrow inlet surrounded by steep hills. We drop anchor near Lazareto Island at the edge of the town. The island is tiny and covered in pine trees and we read it was once used as a quarantine station. In the centre, and nestled amongst the pines, is the chapel of the Transfiguration of the Saviour. We swim ashore to have a look. The church is locked but through the window we can see piles of prayerbooks and a cabinet of relics. There's one other boat near us and it's good not to have to worry about taking lines ashore. We can't get away from the wind, however. It comes tearing over the hillside in katabatic blasts and in the afternoon El Oro strains one way and the other against her anchor chain. Fortunately, the holding is good and although we surge around in all directions the anchor holds.

I take our transit log ashore to get it stamped by the port police. The crew has changed several times since this was originally issued in Corfu and I'm a bit worried we're going to be in trouble for having the wrong crew list on the log. The official behind the desk looks at my document and says, 'Five people on board? Two UK and 3 Australians?'

'Erm yes, that's right' I say, omitting to mention they don't happen to be the same two English and three Australians who are listed on the transit log. He stamps the form and hands it back.

On Thom's recommendation we head back across to the other side of the Inland Sea to Kalamos. There's one small harbour halfway along the island and the tattered pilot book we have on board, dated 2012, recommends booking into George's restaurant. I call them up and am told George will help us into the wharf.

Sure enough, George is waiting on the quay when we arrive and, waving his arms imperiously, issues instructions where to drop our anchor and where we should secure our stern. He's an imposing figure who spends a lot of the day directing traffic in and out of the harbour. He also seems to be the self-styled mayor of the island. There are a couple of other restaurants around the waterfront but as all visiting traffic is met by George, they must struggle to get much patronage. We find ourselves parked next to a group of Italian boys on a highly varnished timber sloop. They were also our neighbours at Portus Karalis in Cagliari.

Dinner is on the beach, chairs sinking slightly into the pebbles. It's an idyllic setting with the sun disappearing behind the island, the sky turning purple before fading into black. Martin raises his glass and tells us this is the best holiday he's ever had. High praise indeed from a man running a holiday company.

Annabel and Martin leave us the next day and we take the boat into the marina at Lefkada so we can fill up with fuel and do some shopping. It's changeover day for the charter company and the marina is packed with row after row of identical white plastic sloops and catamarans. Cleaning staff swarm over them like ants, carrying packs of clean bedding and swabbing decks. Yacht charter is big business in the Ionian Islands.

With three of us now on board we head to Kastos to try and catch up with our friends again. It's Til's birthday and the sun rises blood red above the hills of mainland Greece. There's a smell of woodsmoke in the air and a hot wind. Short but intense gusts blast down from the hills as if exhaled by a dragon perched somewhere on the heights. They hit the water, darkening the surface and El Oro heels before powering forward. Ross busies himself in the galley preparing a birthday breakfast. We hear muffled curses as he battles to keep the pan on the stove. Later he emerges into the cockpit, red faced and dripping with sweat but triumphantly bearing eggs and bacon. As we head south, past Meganisi and around the northern tip of Kalamos the smoke thickens and for a while we can barely see a few metres in front of us. We're in a world of our own navigating from the GPS. Occasionally yachts emerge from the gloom, sails reefed in the strong wind, only to disappear back into the smog. It's almost apocalyptic; we don't see any flames, but the hills above the Inland Sea must be ablaze. Later we discover the fires are hundreds of miles away, the other side of Greece, but we are caught in their massive plume of smoke.

It's not far to Kastos and soon after we come around the north-eastern tip of the narrow island and motor along the southern side. There's not much sign of life. A series of bays with barren looking rock and scrub rising to a low ridgeline. There's a small town also called Kastos, and we anchor in a sheltered cove outside the little fishing harbour. There are a few other yachts here, including our friends, but it's not crowded which makes a refreshing change. We wander back from the waterfront and up the hill behind the town which is no more than a couple of streets deep. The pace of life seems slower here. We mutter 'kalimera' to a small group of men, perhaps employed by the local council, leaning on their shovels around an open drain. Fortunately, the smoke has cleared a little although the locals are nervous about fire. They tell us there's no firefighting equipment on the island.

After a pleasant evening celebrating Til's birthday at the Windmill Taverna on the hill above Kastos, we head off in the morning for Fiskardo on Cephalonia. This is a notoriously busy spot, and we're keen to get there early before the crowds. It's a three-hour motor across flat calm water and we track back past some familiar sights. Kalamos slides past to our north and later we pass the beautiful island of Atokos which sits in the middle of the Inland Sea and is famous for the wild pigs living there. We see them through binoculars, a small group of dark brown adults and some piglets rootling around on the edge of the beach. From there we skirt the northern tip of Ithaka, a large white superyacht moored beneath the rugged cliffs that plunge sheer into the water. We cross the narrow passage over to Cephalonia, largest of the islands in this area, and make our way into Fiskardo.

We've arrived at the right time as there's a stream of yachts heading in the other direction and there's plenty of room. We moor up with little difficulty, stern to the pine trees on the northern side of the narrow bay. It fills up later in the day and the breeze also springs up making anchoring tricky. We watch the ensuing chaos smugly.

A huge grey charter catamaran comes in one side of us. There's a professional crew on board and they bustle around in their matching grey uniforms making their guests comfortable. The girls wear the shortest of miniskirts and look great, but it doesn't seem very practical boat wear. On the other side we have a boat full of German nudists. There are three generations and only the children wear any clothes. We get to see a lot more of Grandpa than we need to. There's not much room between us, but at dusk, a large plastic catamaran tries to push its way in. It's full of Italians and there's a lot of shouting among them as they try and manoeuvre their un-manoeuvrable vessel into the tight spot. It takes them a few goes and at one point they are sideways on, pressed hard against our anchor chain. More shouting and handwaving, they manage to free themselves without too much scraping and unabashed they line up for another try. This time they manage to squeeze in, our fenders bulging as they press tightly against us.

Ashore, I take the opportunity to get the crew list right on the transit log as there's a friendly port police lady. I create a new crew list all neatly lined and draw an intricate ship's logo on the top of the page and ask her to stamp it so it's official. She says she can't unless she sees all the crew in person. No problem, I say and call them in as Til and Ross are waiting outside the door. She gives it the official stamp of approval and we're legal once again.

Fiskardo lives up to its reputation for beauty, and we're in a secure anchorage, so we stay for a few days. There's a walking track through the trees behind our berth winding around the headland past a ruined priory; a scent of pine needles in the air and a soft carpet of them underfoot. There are glimpses of the water through the trees; it's a magical place.

Before leaving, we catch up briefly for an early morning coffee with an Australian friend, Rob and his daughter Willa who are on holiday in Cephalonia. Rob moved to the UK some years ago and has set up a chain of coffee shops in the Cotswolds. We sit on the boat in the early morning light, chatting about the business and what he's achieved. He's been very successful, but it's come at a cost as it's stressful and exhausting. He tells us escaping on a yacht for a year sounds very appealing!

Tim tries to persuade us to stay longer on El Oro. Over email he tells us we've barely scratched the surface of the Mediterranean, there's so much more to explore. We know he's right, but we've already been away for a year, and we need to get home to try and earn some money. We also need to leave the European Schengen zone as our 90-day visa is about to expire. When I explain this, he writes back suggesting Turkey is nice at this time of year, or perhaps we could go further afield. 'If I was a young man again,' he writes, 'I'd head for Sri Lanka. You can have a good life there,' signing off with his trademark, 'Do not hurry, life is not a rehearsal.' It's a bit surreal having this open-ended offer. It's tempting, but although we've met a lot of people spending a lifetime travelling the waterways of the world it's not something we want to do for ever. Feeling as if we're letting Tim and ourselves down, we politely decline, and end up agreeing we'll leave the boat in Sicily where it will over-winter next to Four Seasons.

We're in our last days in Greece now and we try and drink in every minute of it. In glassy conditions we motor north past the familiar Lefkas coastline back to the anchorage outside of Ligia. From there I take the dinghy and power up the canal to Lefkada carving a perfect vee through the flat water. I'm there to pick up 23-year-old Alice. She's the daughter of Liz and Adam who were with us a couple of months ago. It was her friend Tom who sailed with us from Gibraltar to Sardinia, so we assume he must have passed on a favourable report about his time on El Oro. Alice hasn't done a lot of sailing, but she seems unfazed by the idea of the crossing to Sicily.

A couple of days later I'm zipping through the canal in the inflatable once again. This time it's 11.00pm and I have the portable red and green navigation lights clamped onto the bow as I carve through the darkness. It's pitch black, the moon is not yet out, and I follow the lights of the channel markers through the empty waterway. Dominic is waiting at the marina. He's another repeat customer on El Oro; he and Shoonagh joined us for a week in the Caribbean in February when we were mired in problems with the propeller and the windlass.

SEPTEMBER

In the morning we motor back up the channel to do some last-minute shopping and go through the clearance process. We also pick up Thom, the Dutch charter skipper who has agreed to come with us for the trip across the Ionian Sea. He has no charterers this week and is keen to get some more offshore sailing experience. This means we now have six on board so can comfortably run three watches and get a bit more sleep.

There's the familiar bureaucratic dance to be done checking out from the country and we go to the port police first before being directed to customs. There's a bit of a drama there with our paperwork; once again it seems I don't have the right authority to skipper the boat. After the incident in Corfu, Tim sent an email confirming I have the authority to operate El Oro, which I forwarded on to the Corfu customs official. I never heard anything back so assumed it must be OK. Now trying to leave, the customs official in Lefkada tells me an email isn't sufficient documentation. I tell her it was good enough for the Corfu officials and she shakes her head and rolls her eyes. I'm not sure if she's intimating her colleagues in Corfu are misguided or whether it's me. There's a bit of a standoff with lots of tutting from her side and apologetic shoulder shrugging from mine and for a while it seems we're going nowhere. I promise to have this rectified next time I come into the country and eventually she gives up the battle. She's made her point, and with a flourish of the stamp pad we're cleared out.

It turns out the swing bridge across the canal which opens on the hour is closed for lunch at 1.00pm so we shoot for the 2.00pm exit slot. There's the usual jostling as we approach and when the bridge opens, a flood of boats pushes through. We weave our way through the narrow passage, around the sandbanks off the northern end and finally we're out into clear water on our way to Sicily.

The forecast shows headwinds for the next few days and sure enough, we're hard on the breeze heading slightly south of west as we gradually pull away from Lefkas. It takes a long time for the high ground to fade from view, but as the evening draws on, the land disappears into the haze and we gradually get headed. We're going to have to tack our way across the Ionian Sea. The wind builds steadily, and we make uncomfortable and slow progress across the chart, at times pointing towards the toe of Italy before tacking back towards North Africa. We keep one engine on to give us a bit more lift, but our tacking angles are still atrocious and it's difficult to make headway upwind. The seas are steep and short; classic Mediterranean 'square waves' and they push us off our course as well as stopping us dead. The interval between them is short and the motion is uncomfortable and tiring. Dominic succumbs first to seasickness and later Til is also vomiting. It's the first time she's been sick on the entire voyage.

It's 275 nautical miles to Syracuse but we end up doing nearer 400 as we zig zag our way across the Ionian. Late in the afternoon, 48 hours after leaving Lefkas, we spot land; the southern tip of Calabria, the toe of Italy. We tack back and at last get a favourable breeze out of the straits of Messina and finally we can head directly towards our destination. Still well out to sea, Alice spots a floating paddleboard complete with paddle neatly tucked under some elastic straps. We divert slightly and pick it up – it's almost brand new and must have blown off the beach nearly twenty miles away. Someone would have been awfully disappointed to have lost it.

That night, our third out from Lefkas, the breeze drops to nothing, and we motor southwest gradually closing the coast. The vast shape of Mt Etna outlined in the moonlight for a while before it disappears back into cloud and darkness. Eventually we pick up the loom of light from Syracuse and an hour later motor cautiously between the headlands into the wide, sheltered bay arriving at 3.00am. It's been a hard crossing and it's a wonderful relief to drop anchor.

In the morning the view is spectacular. Syracuse is laid out in front of us, the sandstone buildings golden in the low sunlight. Much of it dates from Roman times or earlier and the island of Ortigia with its ancient buildings and narrow laneways is enticing. The holding seems good, so after cleaning up the mess caused by the tough few days at sea we head ashore to explore. Reputedly there is a church containing a painting by Caravaggio, but the relevant section is closed when we're there. Ortigia is touristy but stunning, the architecture unchanged since ancient times. We have lunch in a narrow laneway and at one stage a wedding party squeezes past, the bride in gauzy layers of white chiffon, her bridesmaid carrying her long train behind her.

Dominic gets on the bus to the airport having rolled up and squeezed two paddleboards into his bag. He and Shoonagh bought us one when they joined in St Lucia, and he now also takes the board we reclaimed from the sea. As Alice was the one who spotted it, he pays her a finder's fee of €100 which helps soften the blow of her pricy airfare out of Sicily. Thom also leaves us as he has new charterers joining at the weekend. He makes his way back to Lefkas via a tortuous journey that takes him by air to Athens followed by a long coach ride across Greece. It will take him almost as long to get back as it did to sail here.

Four of us remain and we pull the anchor up early the next morning for our final sail on El Oro. The breeze is light and favourable, and we hoist the mizzen and big grey genoa as we follow the coastline round to Marina di Ragusa. Unlike the north of the island, which is high and mountainous, this part of Sicily is flat and agricultural. Acres of polytunnels cover the ground and we imagine they contain giant forests of tomatoes and aubergines.

It's about 60 miles to our destination and it's late afternoon before we arrive. Approaching Ragusa, we are passed by a yacht heading the other way. A few moments later, Til's phone pings, and there's an Instagram message with video footage of El Oro slicing through the waves. They must have seen our name on the AIS and then looked us up. Coming into the marina we have the usual tricky entry as the breeze has built during the day, but we negotiate the fuel wharf and our final berth with no real problems, helped by marineros in dinghies who push our stern into place.

From here it's a whirlwind of packing and cleaning. Alice leaves us for Seville in the morning and Ross heads off the next day. We meet Sam who Kent has organised to keep an eye on the boat when we leave. He's a softly spoken, laid-back Englishman who speaks with a 'mongrel Devon' accent, as he describes it. He washed up in Sicily after sailing the world in a homemade boat and lives here now, married to a local.

And just like that our trip comes to an end. We do a last-minute polish; I leave a few notes for Kent and at 5.00am on 5 September we put in the washboards for the last time and step ashore to catch the early bus to Catania.

It's strange stepping off El Oro. She's been our home for a year, but she's also been much more than that. She's taken us safely thousands of miles, from one side of the world to another. Sailors have often considered their ships living beings, and it's easy to see why. When you're away from land, you depend utterly on your vessel to keep you safe. It's natural to personify yachts and we've become very attached to El Oro. I've slept aboard every night for a year, and Til's done almost the same. We've become attuned to every creak and groan from the hull or the rig, ready to jump up at once if something's amiss. El Oro's a difficult boat to sail and needs lots of people to manage her, but she's also a beautiful, seaworthy yacht and she's brought us safely home.

Over the year, we've been challenged by a litany of problems. We've battled with the hydraulic steering, we've had total electrical failure, plumbing disasters, various mechanical problems, a propellor blade has fallen off, we almost lost the boat when the seal on the propeller shaft failed, not to mention endless battles with the windlass. We've learned so much, but more than anything we've learned about people. A boat at sea is like a pressure cooker. If you put a group of people into a confined space, and subject them to some stress, it can bring things to the boil. Add in some alcohol from time to time and the pressure ratchets up further. It's impossible to maintain a façade for long on a boat and if there's an issue brewing, it will come to the fore sooner or later. It's a credit to the calibre of people who joined us that this happened only rarely. We had sixty-five people join us on El Oro throughout the year, many of whom were not sailors. Some had a relaxing holiday in the sun, but for others the experience was more challenging. We couldn't sail El Oro by ourselves, so we had to learn how to manage the human relationships to be able to work the boat successfully. It perhaps sounds trite, but when people came on board, we asked them to bring their best self, and we asked the same of ourselves.

⎈

A few weeks after getting back to Australia, there's a message from my sister, Leafy. She's been contacted on Facebook by someone called Vadim who she doesn't know. Vadim is the captain of a tanker crossing the Atlantic and they have come across an abandoned yacht drifting on the ocean. It's Le Chercheur, still afloat, and with AIS still operating, four months after we last saw it. He sends Leafy a screenshot of the AIS plot showing the latitude and longitude. It's only moved 150 miles from where we left it. He also sends a video clip. Le Chercheur looks a little bedraggled, the main has come away from the mast and the boom is dragging in the water, but the hull is floating high. Without talking to the owners, it's impossible to know what happened, but it wasn't sinking. The family on board must have been terrified to take the risk of abandoning ship mid ocean. It's no small thing to climb up the side of a tanker with two small children.

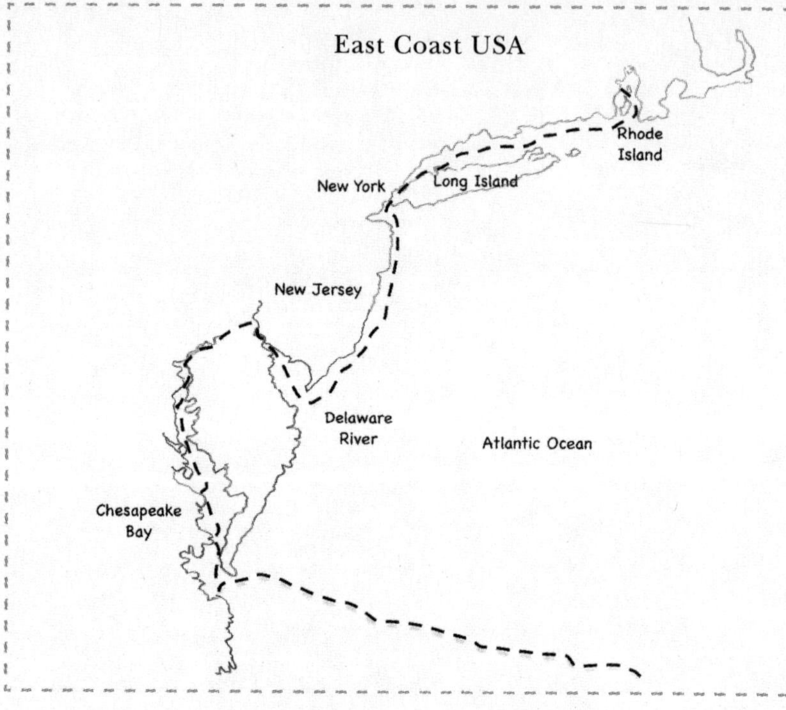
East Coast USA
Rhode Island
Long Island
New York
New Jersey
Delaware River
Atlantic Ocean
Chesapeake Bay

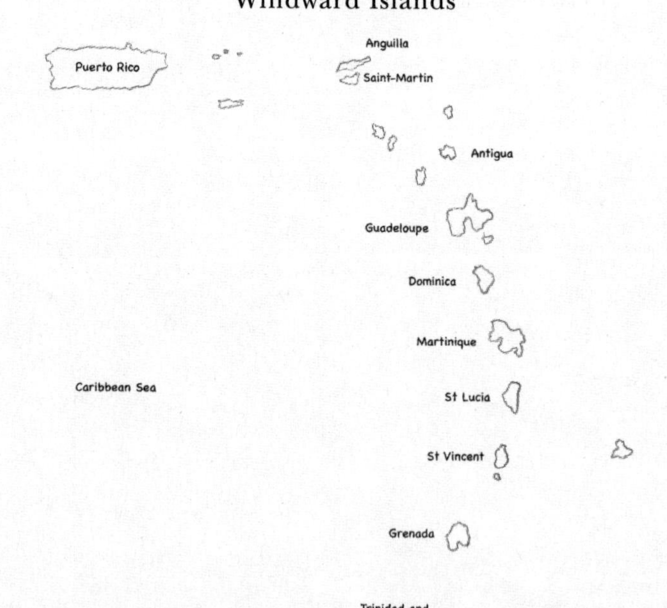
Windward Islands
Anguilla
Puerto Rico
Saint-Martin
Antigua
Guadeloupe
Dominica
Martinique
Caribbean Sea
St Lucia
St Vincent
Grenada
Trinidad and Tobago

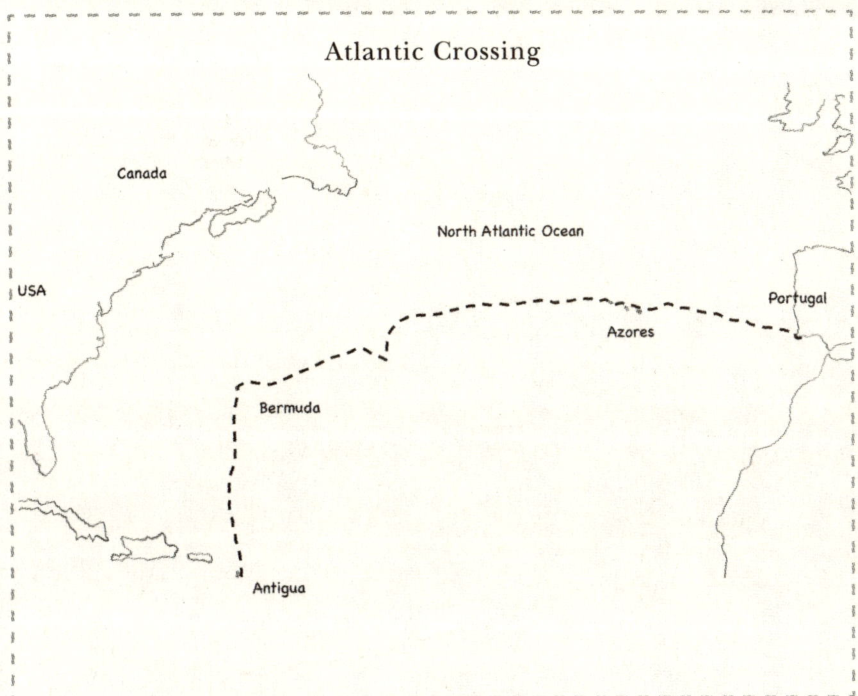

Atlantic Crossing

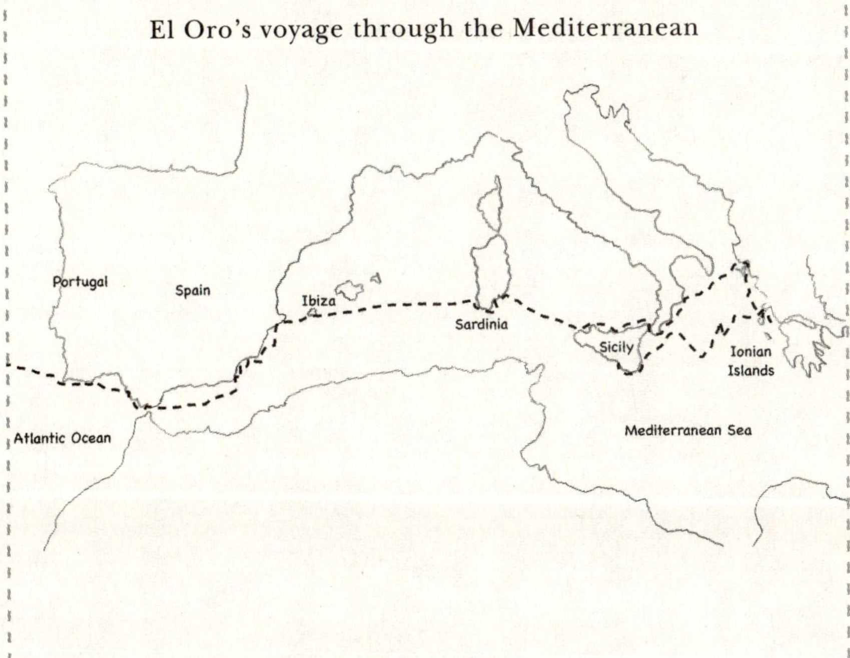

El Oro's voyage through the Mediterranean